TALES
OF
MICHIGAN
II

Constance M. Jerlecki

INLAND
EXPRESSIONS

Clinton Township, Michigan

Published by Inland Expressions

Inland Expressions
42211 Garfield Rd. #297
Clinton Township, MI. 48038

www.inlandexpressions.com

First Edition 2015

CS060916

ISBN-13 978-1-939150-17-2

Printed in the United States of America.

Design by Inland Expressions

Front Cover: As a schooner continues its journey under full sail on the Lake
Michigan horizon, a coal-fired tugboat steams its way into Charlevoix under a
heavy exhaust plume.

Table of Contents

Preface..i

Chapter One
An Inferno on Woodward Avenue—1894 1

Chapter Two
Michigan's Fish Cars—1888-1938 7

Chapter Three
Stout Air Services 1926-1930..18

Chapter Four
A Simple Misunderstanding 28

Chapter Five
Captain Curtis Boughton—1813-1896 35

Chapter Six
Tragic Oversight—1926...40

Chapter Seven
Alpena's Great Fire of 1872 50

Chapter Eight
The Balkan Mine Disaster—1914 56

Chapter Nine
Cholera Epidemic at Detroit—1832 60

Chapter Ten
Dog Sled Teams of the Upper Peninsula.........................66

Chapter Eleven
Grand Rapids Tornado—1912..73

Chapter Twelve
Deadly Windfall 78

Chapter Thirteen
Disaster on Easter Sunday 91

Chapter Fourteen
Abraham Lincoln Visits Kalamazoo 101

Chapter Fifteen
The St. Clair Tunnel—1891 110

Notes 125

Bibliography 139

Index 143

Table of Contents

Preface

In keeping with the theme established with the initial book in this series, a decision was made to incorporate a broad range of stories from across the state rather than concentrating on any single aspect of Michigan's history or geographical region. Therefore, each of the following chapters focuses on one particular subject matter, with an emphasis, in most cases, placed upon relating lesser known events and individuals that are components of Michigan's historical heritage.

The efficient movement of people and goods has always played a prominent role in the economic and cultural development of the state. As such, several of the following accounts concern a number of transportation methods ranging from dog sled teams to air travel. With a rich maritime heritage, it should come as no surprise that several of the tales included in this volume of Michigan history incorporate nautical themes. This latter transportation method led to one of the strangest episodes in the history of the Great Lakes region when the grounding of a gasoline-laden tanker in northern Lake Michigan led to a frenzied, but dangerous, effort by the local population to retrieve the valuable fuel.

Rail traffic also contributed greatly to the economic and population growth of Michigan. As related in the following pages, this mode of transportation played a key role in the development of the state's commercial fishing industry along with the creation of an extensive rail network that provided several communities with a safe and dependable form of travel long before automobile ownership became commonplace. In addition, Michigan's unique geographic location with the nation's northern neighbor led to the construction of a groundbreaking international rail tunnel that paid huge dividends for over one-hundred years.

While the fifteen stories included in this book can only scratch the surface of Michigan's rich and varied past, it is hoped that the reader gains an additional insight into the story of the "Great Lakes State" through the reading of this book.

Constance M. Jerlecki
April 2015

i

Chapter One
An Inferno on Woodward Avenue - 1894

As the sun rose into the skies above Detroit on the autumn morning of Friday October 5, 1894, the Keenan & Jahn furniture store on Woodward Avenue came to life as workers began their daily toils. At approximately 7:30 a.m. that morning, employees working in a shipping room located in the basement of the five-story building discovered a fire in a pile of wood shavings.[1] Growing quickly as it sought to consume the highly combustible material, the small blaze soon blossomed into a raging inferno. As the alarm sounded, the sixty workers inside the store began a desperate struggle to escape the burning building.

Upon reaching the elevator shaft, the fire began spreading upwards throughout the old building. As the smoke and flames pushed their way into every corner of their workplace, many of the fleeing employees encountered great difficulty in making their escape.[2] Despite the obstacles, everyone managed to reach the relative safety offered by the streets outside. Once there, however, the workers could do little more than await the arrival of the fire department.

Arriving within minutes of receiving the call, firefighters found the fire had gained significant headway during its unabated march through the furniture store. As such, when the first streams of water erupted from the fire hoses, the building's upper floors were already fully ablaze.[3] Even as firefighters continued their efforts to subdue the conflagration from Woodward Avenue and an alley at the rear of the furniture store, some of their comrades began the dangerous task of forcing their

1

way inside the burning structure.[4]

Given the scope of the task, these efforts proved remarkably successful with the blaze largely contained within an hour's time. Despite this, however, the fire had badly damaged the floors and wooden joists that made up the building's internal structure. Contemporary accounts of the disaster describe the intensity of the inferno sufficient to cause the exterior walls to radiate waves of heat similar to those from a furnace. Just a few minutes before 9 o'clock that morning, several fire fighters stationed at the front of the smoldering building were ordered into windows on the second floor to assist in extinguishing the last remaining pockets of fire.[5]

Ascending ladders to reach their assigned positions, the men had no way of knowing their lives and those of their fellow firefighters below were in imminent danger. Above their heads on the roof of Keenan & Jahn's furniture store at that particular moment, the supports holding the elevator trunk were about to give way after being damaged by the fire. Installed long after the building's original construction, the elevator mechanism had never received adequate support. Without warning, the heavy piece of equipment tore loose from its precarious mounting to begin its downward crash.[6]

The pressures exerted upon the fire damaged structure as the mass of steel and cables fell downwards through the five floors below forced the building's exterior walls to buckle outwards. Unable to withstand such forces in its weakened condition, the front of furniture store started to come apart as it began its collapse towards Woodward Avenue. While warnings shouted to the firefighters just moments before the front wall tumbled down allowed many of their number to escape injury, for some it was too late.

The excitement of the fire had attracted a large number of curious spectators. As the wall tore itself to pieces, the large crowd scattered to put as much distance between itself and the furniture store. While many made mad dashes through the city streets, others sought refuge inside nearby businesses. During the melee, the panicked crowd trampled several people, including a number of children. As can be expected, numerous bystanders received injuries during the stampede, none of which proved to be serious.[7]

Back at the front of Keenan & Jahn's furniture store, however, the story was very different. During its final plummet, the material making up the building's front wall carried anyone caught in its path into the street below. Within seconds, a large pile of debris consisting of bricks, wood, glass, and broken bodies had risen several feet above the sidewalk bordering Woodward Avenue. During the collapse, a portion of the building's front wall severed a series of power lines running along the street. The sparks and smoke generated by the downed cables briefly added a further element of danger to the confused scene.[8]

Seconds after the wall completed its disintegration, firefighters rushed back to the front of the now demolished furniture store to begin the effort to rescue anyone trapped inside the smoking wreckage. While the vast majority of those present managed to escape injury, it was inevitable that others were not as lucky. In total, sixteen men were caught up by the collapse. The first body recovered from the wreckage was that of Lieutenant Michael H. Donaghue of Chemical No. 1. As the search continued, the next two victims located both came from Engine No. 9, these being pipemen Joseph R. Dely and John W. Pagel.[9] A short time later, searchers pulled the badly crushed body of Julius G. Cummings from the ruins. Although recovery personnel discovered the shattered helmet belonging to fireman Martin Ball on the morning of the disaster, it would not be until later that afternoon that his body was found buried beneath twelve feet of debris.[10]

3

An early twentieth century view of Woodward Avenue. (Library of Congress)

In addition to these five victims, rescuers also pulled the badly mangled body of Fred J. Bussey from the rubble. Barely alive when found, Bussey was a spectator acting as a volunteer firefighter. Rushed to Grace Hospital, the critically injured man died a short time later. Although not a member of the Detroit Fire Department, Bussey is considered as being one of the firefighters killed that October morning.

Other than the six fatalities, the wall collapse also left ten other firefighters with wounds ranging from minor bruising to serious head and internal injuries. The injured included Lieutenant Patrick O'Rourke, Bartholomew Cronin, Fred Draheim, Michael C. Gray, Thomas Gurry, Henry Herig, Leslie E. McElmurray, John B. Newell, E. E. Stevens, and F. E. Stocks.[11] Although doctors had initially expressed serious doubts as to whether certain of these individuals would survive, all of those injured eventually recovered. Despite this outcome, many of these men carried the scars of that morning throughout the balance of their lives.[12]

As can be expected from such tragedies, it did not take long for those in charge to come under fire in the press. By the afternoon of October 5, 1894, news reports criticizing Chief James R. Elliot began appearing in the evening editions of local newspapers. Within twenty-four hours, word of the tragedy had spread across the nation as other news outlets picked up the story. Indicative of the incriminations leveled at Chief Elliot in the immediate aftermath of the fire, the following excerpt comes from the October 6, 1894 edition of New York City's *The World*:

> Chief Elliot, of the Fire Department is much criticised [*sic*] for ordering his men into the building at the front entrance when he probably knew the walls were unsafe. Elliott replies that the firemen were sent where duty required.

Following the fire, the loss of which amounted to approximately $85,000, the firm of Keenan & Jahn moved to a new building located at 334 Woodward. Born in 1841, James J. Keenan first arrived in Detroit around 1861. After working briefly at the Michigan Exchange as a night watchman he found employment painting chairs at the Detroit Chair Company. After spending three further years in the furniture business, Keenan tried his hand at running a hotel. This proving unsuccessful, he later found a job buying produce for a local firm before taking a position at a furniture store named P. Hufnagle & Co. in February of 1869. Three years later, Keenan, along with two other associates, formed the Kirchberg, Winterhalter, & Keenan furniture house. In 1887, James Keenan and Adolph Jahn bought out the other members of the firm to establish the Keenan & Jahn furniture store.

James J. Keenan died on April 21, 1919 at the age of seventy-eight. During his life, Keenan had two sons, James and Joseph, and one daughter. His burial took place at Detroit's Mt. Elliot

Cemetery.[13]

After relying upon volunteer fire companies for several years, the city of Detroit purchased a steam fire engine and hired its first paid firefighters in 1860. Given the dangers involved in its task, it is unsurprising that the Detroit Fire Department has suffered occasional losses throughout its 150-year history. At times, these tragic events have resulted in multiple deaths among the Department's personnel. This all too lengthy list includes a structural collapse on March 4, 1917 that killed five firefighters battling a blaze in two downtown buildings occupied by the Field's Cloak & Suit Company and the R. H. Fyfe Shoe Company.[14] More recently, a pair of warehouse fires on the city's west side that took place on March 12, 1987 resulted in the deaths of three fire fighters.[15] Despite these incidents, the fire at Keenan & Jahn's furniture store on October 5, 1897 remains the darkest day in the history of the Detroit Fire Department.

Chapter Two
Michigan's Fish Cars – 1888-1938

The passage of Public Act No. 124 by the Michigan Legislature in early 1873 resulted in the establishment of the Michigan Fish Commission Board. On April 19 of that year Governor John J. Bagley, George Clark of Ecorse, and George H. Jerome of Niles became the commission's first members, the latter of which later became the state's first chief of fisheries. The establishment of the commission did not come about to promote sport or recreational fishing, but rather the stocking of the state's waterways with a dependable supply of food. As such, one of its primary duties was the propagation of whitefish—one of the most important food fishes in the Great Lakes region.[1]

By the dawn of the 1870s, state officials recognized the growing disparity between the yields of food cultivation on land to those from water. Whereas farming had benefited from a series of technological progresses to improve its efficiency and output, the stability of the fish supply in the state's waterways had been largely ignored.[2] This shortcoming along with the indifferent attitude of the commercial fishing firms operating in the freshwater expanses of the Great Lakes had sparked a steady decline in the numbers of annual fish harvests. Reflecting upon this situation, the commission's twelfth biennial report released in 1897 contained the following statement, "The history of commercial fishing in the [G]reat [L]akes for the past twenty-five years is the history of an abuse." Expanding upon its criticism of the commercial fishing industry, the report continued with, "The people of the State are more deeply interested in the preservation

7

of the [G]reat [L]ake fisheries than the person who draws from them the product that gives him his daily bread."[3]

The Michigan Fish Commission established its first fish hatchery on a piece of land it leased in Cass County on October 1, 1873. Located about six miles from Niles at Crystal Springs, the site was about half that distance from the Michigan Central Railroad's Pokagon station. In addition to a hatchery measuring 20 feet by 60 feet in size, other work done at this location included the construction of several ponds and a residence for the facility's manager. In 1879, this hatchery produced the first brook trout planted by the commission, the distribution of which took place at six locations within Berrien, Cass, and Kalamazoo counties.[4]

In the same year that Michigan created its board of fish commissioners, Dr. Livingston Stone conducted a series of experiments transporting fry (newly hatched fish) for the U.S. Fish Commission. Involving trips between the East and West coasts, Dr. Stone worked laboriously to develop the techniques necessary to ship live fish by rail. During transport, the water in the fish cans required constant aeration and changing to keep it free of impurities. As cold water better absorbed oxygen and reduced the stress placed on the fish, these trials also demonstrated the importance of using ice to cool the water.

To transport young fish from the hatcheries to areas for planting, the Michigan Fish Commission relied upon the various railroads operating throughout the state. The most important of these during the early years of such operations was the Michigan Central Railroad, the lines of which served the hatchery operations at Detroit and Pokagon. In its 1876 biennial report, the commission paid special tribute to the railroads for moving their cans of fish and attendants free of charge, thus allowing the successful planting of fish in nearly every county in the state.

In addition to recognizing the contributions made by the

railway companies, the same report also praised others for their assistance in carrying out successful fish plants during the previous two years. This included the Tug Association of Detroit, which, through the offices of Captain Drummond, provided the tugboat *William Livingstone* from which the commission was able to plant approximately one-million fish across several miles of the Detroit River. Additional deposits during 1876 included upwards to 600,000 fish in Lake Michigan between Grand Haven and Saugatuck Point, and similar plants in Lake Erie. In a practice common with that of the railroads, the owners of the vessels involved in these operations provided their use to the commission free of charge.[5]

An inadequate supply of water forced the closure of the Pokagon station in 1881. Following the conclusion of an extensive search, the State Board of Fish Commissioners decided in July of that year to construct a new hatchery at Paris in Mecosta County. On this site, which was located on a tributary of the Muskegon River named Cheney Creek, work soon began on a new 20 by 60 foot hatchery. Before the year was out, further construction saw the completion of several ponds and a home for the hatchery's overseer. By 1887, demands placed upon the facility prompted the construction of a second, and larger, hatchery building.[6]

Since its inception, the commission had identified a need to acquire its own fish railcar. Under the established guidelines, the movement of fish relied upon the generosity of the railroad companies to provide cars during the planting season, which coincided with their busiest months of the year. This situation placed the railroads in the unfavorable position of trying to provide space during its most profitable season. As such, many of the cars allocated to this task where often found to be in various states of disrepair. As these cars traveled with passenger trains running on tight schedules, the discovery of any

The main building of the Paris fish hatchery in Mecosta County as it appeared circa 1910. (Author's Collection)

deficiencies at any point along the route brought the danger of its removal from the train.

In the spring of 1888, an incident occurred during one of these movements that underscored the hazards associated with the commission transporting its perishable cargoes within the current framework. When railroad officials inspecting a railcar carrying a cargo estimated to contain between two and three million fry found it in a deplorable condition, they threatened to remove it from the train. Through a series of telegraph messages, however, the employees in charge of the car convinced the railroad officials to allow the railcar to continue its journey. While this solution prevented the loss of the perishable cargo, it nonetheless highlighted the commission's vulnerability of relying upon the railroads to provide space for its annual shipments.[7]

The lack of a dedicated fish car also precluded the distribution of certain species of fish. This included the German carp and walleyed pike, the planting of which required parties desiring these fish to bear the burden of either traveling to a hatchery or paying for express transportation services. Without its own railcar, the commission was also ill-equipped to redistribute the black bass from areas in which they were abundant to those where their numbers had been depleted.[8]

In 1887, Congress passed the Interstate Commerce Act in an effort to curb the growing power of the railroads. Uncertain of how the new regulations would affect their business, all of the railroads involved in moving fish plants informed the fish commission they would no longer issue free passes to the attendants accompanying these cargoes. To cover the anticipated expenses, the state legislature appropriated an additional $6,000 to the commission's budget. As the excitement over the new federal regulations subsided, however, a number of the railroads reinstated the free pass system, a practice soon followed by most others across the state.[9]

With the entire $6,000 appropriation no longer needed to cover the increased traveling expenses, the commission seized the opportunity to use this money to finance the acquisition of a dedicated fish car. Finding all of the railcar manufacturers in the state unable to accept a contract due to having too much work, the commission entered into an agreement with the Litchfield Car Company of Litchfield, Illinois for the construction of a fish car for $3,550—a sum $1,000 lower than the next lowest bidder.[10]

Measuring 55 feet in length and 9 feet 8 inches in width, the fish car was equipped with an office in one end and a kitchen in the other. These facilities, along with five sleeping berths, allowed the men accompanying the fish cargoes to live aboard the dedicated car, thereby significantly reducing the commission's travel expenses. Installed along each side of a center aisle was a series of lockers equipped with wooden covers to hold three rows of 10-gallon fish cans.[11] This arrangement permitted the fish car to carry up to 175 cans of fry, a number significantly higher than previously possible by appropriating available space in baggage cars. By acquiring its own fish car, the commission also eliminated its reliance upon the railroads for issuing free passes to its workers accompanying the fish cargoes.[12]

Its construction completed, the commission took delivery of the fish car from the Litchfield Car Company on August 1, 1888. Named *Attikumaig*—the Chippewa name for whitefish as related by geologist Henry Schoolcraft—the words MICHIGAN FISH COMMISSION adorned each side of the car in large gold letters. Although equipped with large side doors to facilitate the loading and unloading of fish cans, the car featured a window pattern that resulted in it having an outward appearance similar to those of contemporary passenger coaches.[13]

While the Litchfield Company demonstrated great efficiency by delivering the car within the terms of its contract, the lateness of the season precluded its heavy use during its first year of operation. This, however, did not prevent the commission from distributing approximately 1,600 black bass that year. Reporting this fact in its eighth biennial report, the commission predicted dramatic increases in the efficiency of fish plants in the coming years.[14]

The demands placed upon the *Attikumaig* by the commission are evident by the number of miles it traveled during its first full year of operation. In 1889, the fish car traveled 18,731 miles between February 15 and June 10 of that year alone. With an additional 2,000 miles added by special trips, the *Attikumaig* traversed in excess of 20,000 miles before the end of the year. This respectable tabulation gains more significance by the fact that all of the fish car's travels took place within the borders of Michigan. During 1890, the *Attikumaig* accumulated a mileage of just over 16,300 miles while two other cars engaged by the commission added an additional 5,432 miles to that year's total.[15]

Besides offering increased flexibility and greater efficiencies, the operation of a dedicated fish car also permitted the fish commission to reduce its operational costs. One such area was the financial outlays associated with feeding the men accompanying the fish plants cargoes. Equipped with its own kitchen facilities, the cook assigned to the *Attikumaig* was able to prepare meals for the crew while the train was en route to and from the planting sites. As calculated by the commission in 1890, the cost of feeding each man aboard the train amounted to $3.50 per week, an amount significantly lower than the previous practice of securing meals at stations along the route.[16]

While the *Attikumaig* proved very effective in its assigned role, the fish commission nonetheless recognized the new railcar still fell short of fulfilling its annual requirements. To this end, its ninth biennial report released in 1890 pointed out this shortcoming by broaching the subject of acquiring a second car. One of the primary obstacles to the *Attikumaig* meeting the commission's needs was the concurrent nature of the whitefish and pikeperch planting seasons. In the spring of 1890, this constraint prompted an arrangement to secure the loan of a fish car from the U.S. Fish Commission along with the renting of an express car from an independent railroad for a period of four weeks.[17] The capacity issues related to operating only one dedicated fish car persisted until being relieved to a significant degree by the opening of a new hatchery at Charlevoix a few years later.

Throughout its practice of securing space aboard regularly scheduled passenger trains, the commission had experienced the occasional missed delivery. The root cause for many of these problems resulted from confusion on the part of the recipients being unable to find which car held their shipments. As the railroads ran on fixed schedules, such instances usually resulted in the train departing the station with the fish still aboard. With the words MICHIGAN FISH COMMISSION emblazoned on its sides, there could be little doubt as to which railcar held the cargo from the hatchery—despite its similar appearance to other cars on the train.[18]

Following seven years of service, the *Attikumaig* received a major overhaul in 1895 at the cost of $1,400. On its first trip following the completion of this project, however, the *Attikumaig* was involved in a serious accident near Traverse City. Thrown from the tracks by a bad switch, the car suffered severe damage when it tumbled down an embankment. Although tossed about by the incident, none of the men aboard the car at the time suffered any serious injuries. In contrast to the crew's lucky escape, the entire cargo of 21,000,000 whitefish eggs destined for the commission's station at Charlevoix was lost.[19]

As the accident resulted from a mistake made by one of its employees, the Chicago & West Michigan Railway (later the Pere Marquette Railway) took the badly damaged fish car to one of its shops for repairs. Although emerging from the repair yard restored to its former appearance, it soon became evident that the accident had weakened the railcar's structure. This condition proved serious enough to necessitate additional repairs to keep it in running order.[20]

It was at some time following the accident that the car was renamed *Fontinalis* in honor of the brook trout.[21] Under its new name, the railcar continued operating until its age and condition forced its retirement in 1912 after having faithfully served the commission for 24 years.

The following year, the state legislature provided the fish commission with a $5,000 appropriation to purchase a new fish car.[22] Discovering this amount was insufficient to finance a newly built car, Superintendent Seymour Bower arranged the purchase of a used Pullman sleeper car for $1,600. He then entered into a contract with Hotchkiss, Blue and Company of Chicago to convert it into a dedicated fish car outfitted in a manner similar to that of the *Fontinalis*.[23]

During the reconstruction process, workers removed all of the sleeper car's lower berths while retaining seven of the upper berths. The car also featured two davenports—one in the dining room and another in the office—that gave it the ability to accommodate a crew of nine men. Besides having a new floor installed, the car also received side doors to facilitate the loading and unloading of the converted milk cans used to transport the fish. The total cost of the project amounted to $3,879—an amount that included a complete overhaul and all of the car's furnishings.[24]

With a length of 81 feet, the *Wolverine* measured 26 feet longer than the *Fontinalis*. Despite its larger size, the refurbished Pullman coach did little to relieve the necessity of securing space

Following an accident near Traverse City, the *Attikumaig* was renamed *Fontinalis* and remained in service until its retirement in 1912. (Author's Collection)

for fish shipments aboard various railroads during the rush season. Outfitted with lockers capable of holding 144 ten-gallon cans of fish and with floor space for 40 more, the new railcar's carrying capacity of 184 cans represented an increase of only 9 cans, or five percent, over its predecessor.[25]

Its reconstruction complete, the *Wolverine* departed the Paris hatchery on Sunday, February 22, 1914 to begin its maiden trip for the commission.[26] When it released its twenty-first biennial report in 1915, the State Board of Fish Commissioners provided a glowing account of its new fish car even while continuing its efforts to secure funding for a second railcar.

Traveling upwards of 25,000 miles each year, the fish cars found their way into nearly every county in Michigan while distributing their cargoes of young fish. Remarkably, the majority of these trips took place within a timeframe consisting of a five-month planting season. For the crews employed aboard the fish cars, life revolved around the safety of their live cargoes, an arduous task requiring them to work a number of hours far in excess than is considered normal today. For example, procedures called for at least one man to be on duty at all times when the car was part of a train or while fish were aboard.[27]

While the commission had found the rails to be a highly effective method in moving its fish cargoes since its earliest days, times were quickly changing by the 1920s. Benefitting from the state's expanding highway system, trucking companies began carrying many of the cargoes formerly handled by the railroads. The opening of new hatcheries compounded this paradigm shift by eliminating the need for many of the longer runs made by the *Wolverine*.

Its usefulness at an end, the fish board's operation of a dedicated fish car concluded on February 2, 1938 when the *Wolverine* departed Paris for the final time. Leaving that small community sixty miles north of Grand Rapids at 4:20 that

Wednesday afternoon, the former Pullman railcar began its sad journey to the scrap yard.[28]

Today, visitors to the Michigan Fisheries Visitors Center located at the Oden State Hatchery just east of Petoskey can tour a replica railcar restored to represent the old *Wolverine* fish car. Based upon a renovated Canadian passenger car, the exhibit is equipped with interactive displays to provide an insight into what life was like for those serving on the railcar during its travels across the state.

Chapter Three
Stout Air Services 1926-1930

On the afternoon of July 31, 1926, a crowd numbering more than 20,000 strong gathered on the grounds of a newly opened airport four miles south of downtown Grand Rapids. During the dedication festivities, officials named the new airfield Daniel Waters Cassard Field in honor of the only Grand Rapids aviator killed in World War I. With the formal dedication of this airport coinciding with the inauguration of air services between that city and the Ford Airport that served Detroit from its location in Dearborn, it was fitting that a Stout 2-AT Air Pullman belonging to the Detroit-Grand Rapids Airline was present at that day's ceremonies. As part of that day's events, Barbara Hill, daughter of Grand Rapids postmaster Robert G. Hill, smashed a bottle of champagne against this aircraft, known as the airline's ship No. 1, thereby christening it the *Miss Grand Rapids*.[1]

Operated by Stout Air Services, the Detroit-Grand Rapids Airline became the first strictly commercial passenger airline in the United States. While the nation could boast as being the birthplace of powered flight, the use of this revolutionary technology for military applications had largely overshadowed the development of commercial aviation during the early twentieth century. In contrast, the same period had witnessed a network of commercial facilities grow to cover nearly the entire continent of Europe prior to the Detroit-Grand Rapids Airline conducting its first revenue flight.[2]

Located a few miles west of downtown Detroit, the Ford Airport was integral to the operation of the Detroit-Grand

Rapids Airline. Besides having hangers to store aircraft operating for Ford's commercial cargo airline, the Ford Air Transport Service, this airport also featured the world's largest airship mooring mast. This latter structure, however, saw little use before that form of aerial transport lost favor to conventionally powered flight.

Intended to be the first step towards the anticipated establishment of a Detroit, St. Paul, and Western airline, the air route between Michigan's largest city and Grand Rapids was purely experimental in nature. The Stout 2-AT Air Pullman employed to carry passengers between these two cities resulted from William Bushnell Stout's belief he could develop an aircraft superior to the biplanes then being used to transport mail across the nation.[3]

Founding the Stout Metal Aircraft Company in 1922, William Stout was among the early aviation pioneers to employ metal rather than fabric to cover an aircraft's structure. Although requiring a higher initial investment, metal required significantly less maintenance than fabric over an aircraft's operational life. One of the early designs to come out of Stout's factory was an all-metal torpedo bomber for the U.S. Navy designated as the ST-1. Following a crash during acceptance trials, however, the government promptly canceled the project.

While William Stout supervised the development of the 2-AT Air Pullman the primary duty of designing the aircraft fell upon his chief engineer, George Prudden. It was during the later stages of this process that Prudden received the assistance of a fellow aeronautical engineer named Thomas Towle. Born in 1887, Towle would go on to figure prominently in the development of the highly successful Ford Tri-Motor.[4]

Following its completion, the prototype 2-AT Air Pullman left Stout's Detroit factory bound for Selfridge Field in nearby Mount Clemens, where it embarked upon its first flight on April 23,

A Stout 2-AT Air Pullman named *Maiden Dearborn* in service with Stout Air Transport. (Library of Congress)

1924. This maiden voyage, however, came to an abrupt end just a few moments after takeoff when a broken windshield forced the pilot to land on a frozen Lake St. Clair. Fortunately, the aircraft sustained no significant damage during the incident and the testing program continued without suffering any serious delays.

Covered with a corrugated metal skin and powered by a 400 horsepower Liberty V12 engine, the Stout 2-AT was able to carry eight passengers in addition to a single pilot. As can be expected with such an innovative design, the type suffered from a number of engineering deficiencies that included, among other things, fatigue cracks. Much to the consternation of its pilots, the inefficiency of the aircraft's large wings in generating lift translated into less than ideal take off characteristics.[5]

Becoming interested in the economic potential of aviation during the early 1920s, Henry Ford began investing in the Stout

Metal Aircraft Company. In early 1925, he convinced William Stout to move his aircraft factory to the Ford Airport. When Ford purchased the company later that same year, it became a division of the Ford Motor Company. Remaining with the company following its acquisition by the automotive giant, William Stout shifted his focus towards developing new designs rather than the actual manufacturing process.

The total production run of the 2-AT Air Pullman amounted to only eleven examples. Of these, five went to the Ford Air Transport Service to carry cargo on the Dearborn to Chicago route, while four others went south to serve with Florida Airways. Of the remaining aircraft, Stout Air Services operated at least one example. Sold for $25,000 each, the innovative nature of the aircraft far exceeded its diminutive production numbers.

By December of 1926, the Detroit-Grand Rapids Airline was operating regularly scheduled flights between Ford Airport and Grand Rapids each day of the week with the exception of Sunday. The fare charged for these journeys amounted to $18 for a one-way flight, and $35 for a round trip ticket. The airline also permitted passengers to purchase a ten-trip book of tickets at a cost of $16 per flight. All of these fares included transportation to and from three selected hotels in each city served by the route.[6] To place these amounts into perspective, the $18 charged for a one-way ticket is equivalent to $241 in 2014.

Despite the higher costs compared to other modes of transport, company brochures emphasized the importance of early reservations as the airline claimed it often faced more demand than available space. This problem was one that also confronted railroad and steamship operators—the two long established public transportation methods of the day.

These same publications included a series of instructions designed to educate a public unfamiliar with the intricacies of passenger flight. A review of this information provides an insight into the standards of early commercial aviation. Included among the entries listed in these pamphlets is a suggestion for travelers to visit the cockpit to discuss the aircraft's controls and navigation instruments with the pilot. While emphasizing the speed and safety of air transport, these company brochures also contained a warning concerning the obvious dangers associated with opening the cabin door before the aircraft had come to complete stop.[7]

In the first seven months of its operation, the Detroit-Grand Rapids Airline carried in excess of 800 passengers with a total traffic load of 150,000 pounds (standard practice in this era was to weigh each passenger before boarding) over a distance exceeding 40,000 miles.[8] With demand remaining steady, the airline reported it had transported nearly 2,000 passengers over an accumulated mileage of 79,636 miles during its first year of operation that ended on July 31, 1927.[9]

On July 27, 1927, Stanley E. Kraus, manager of Stout Air Services, announced the suspension of his company's air service between Detroit and Grand Rapids. This announcement was in line with the reasoning behind the route's original establishment just one year earlier. During an interview given to newspaper reporters, Kraus explained, "We have concluded our experiments and have tested the equipment, rates and schedules on this line." Providing further insight, he continued with, "... and we are now able to base operation on facts and experiences rather than opinion."[10]

While admitting that the revenue generated by the airline during its first year of operation did not fully cover its operating expenses, Mr. Kraus emphasized his company's position by explaining, "...we consider the experience gained more valuable than as if we had made a profit to start with."[11]

Concurrent with the abandonment of its inaugural route, Stout

Air Services announced the creation of a new air service linking Detroit and Cleveland, Ohio. This contrasted sharply with the company's original intention of extending its existing route across Lake Michigan to connect Detroit with Milwaukee and Minneapolis-St. Paul.

Despite having provided steadfast service with a flawless safety record on the Detroit to Grand Rapids route, the 2-AT Air Pullman was becoming increasingly obsolete as newer designs became available. As such, Stout Air Services took the opportunity of introducing the Ford Tri-Motor on its new Detroit -Cleveland route. In any case, the introduction of new federal regulations during 1927 led to the grounding and eventual scrapping of the remaining 2-AT Air Pullmans (one example operated by Ford Air Transport was lost in a 1926 crash).

Tasked with developing a new airliner following Ford's purchase of the Stout Metal Airplane Company, William Stout utilized the 2-AT Air Pullman as the basis for a design powered by three Wright J-4 Whirlwind engines. Designated as the 3-AT, this aircraft flew for the first time in November 1925. When the aircraft's performance failed to live up to expectations, however, a furious Henry Ford replaced Stout in his role as chief engineer of the project with Harold Hicks and Thomas Towle. Despite the loss of the 3-AT prototype in a fire that destroyed the Stout factory at the Ford Airport during the early morning hours of January 17, 1926, the redesign effort proceeded quickly through the early months of that year.

Incorporating a 74-foot wingspan, the revised design featured an engine mounted in the nose and two others in pylons placed along each side of the fuselage and underneath the large overhead wing. As such, the 4-AT-A Ford Tri-Motor could carry up to 8 passengers at a cruising speed of 95 mph over a range of 500 miles. In common with its predecessors, this aircraft also featured a corrugated metal skin that imparted great strength at

23

the cost of increased drag. Therefore, it is unsurprising that the Tri-Motor became commonly referred to as the "Tin Goose," a moniker by which it remains known to this day.

The cabins of the early Tri-Motors utilized by the Detroit-Cleveland Airline were equipped with wicker seats and glass windows that passengers could open or close as desired. Outfitted with heaters for cold weather, these aircraft also featured electric lighting, baggage compartments, and a restroom—amenities future air travelers would take for granted.[12] These luxuries, as they were in the day, allowed passengers—many of which had never flown before—to travel in some level of comfort during their journey between Ford Airport and Cleveland's municipal airport.

By April of 1928, the Detroit-Cleveland Airline was flying four daily flights between Dearborn and Cleveland. This consisted of two morning and two afternoon flights originating from each airport in opposite directions. Regardless of their origin, each of the two aircraft involved departed their respective airfields simultaneously. Rather than taking a direct path over Lake Erie, however, the airliners followed the coastline of Michigan and Ohio to their destinations. Under this arrangement, the Tri-Motors would pass each other somewhere along the shores of the shallowest of the five Great Lakes as they reached the midpoint of the route. The fares charged for these one hour and forty minute flights amounted to $18 for a one-way ticket and $35 for a round trip. In common with the practice established with the Detroit-Grand Rapids route, this service operated daily on a Monday through Saturday schedule.[13]

In an effort to capitalize upon the public's growing fascination with aviation, Stout Air Services began offering sightseeing flights over Detroit. As air travel remained beyond the reach of most people during this era, the $5 ticket price for these excursions allowed many to experience the sensation of flight for the first time. The 25-mile route established by Stout provided passengers aboard its Tri-Motors with a unique view of the various industrial, business, and residential sections of Michigan's largest city.

The combination of its regularly scheduled service and the aerial tour business dramatically increased the number of passengers carried by Stout Air Services on an annual basis. Indicative of this growth is the fact that the company's aircraft handled 46,553 passengers during 1928.[14]

On April 28, 1929, Frederick B. Rentschler, president of the United Aircraft and Transport Corporation, announced his company's acquisition of Stout Air Services. This transaction allowed the growing company, which survives today as United Airlines, to make important connections to Detroit.[15]

Operating as a separate division within the United Aircraft and Transport Corporation, Stout Air Services expanded its operation by opening a route between the Ford Airport and Chicago's

Commonly referred to as the "Tin Goose," the Ford Tri-Motor is one of the most iconic aircraft in the history of aviation. (Library of Congress)

municipal airport with four daily flights. At a cost of $30 for a one-way ticket and $50 for a round-trip, the fares for this route were significantly higher than that charged for the Detroit-Cleveland service, which by July of 1929 had fallen to $14 and $25 for a one-way and round-trip ticket respectively. With a flight time of 1 hour and 50 minutes, the aircraft employed on the Detroit-Chicago route enabled passengers to reach their destinations twice as fast as services offered by express passenger trains.[16]

On December 11, 1929, Stout Air Lines achieved a significant milestone when it carried its 100,000th passenger. This honor went to Michigan Governor Fred W. Green, whom accompanied by company president William B. Stout, flew aboard one of the airline's Tri-Motors from Ford Airport to Cleveland that morning. Interestingly, Governor Green had also been the air service's 50,000th passenger when he embarked upon an excursion flight over Detroit on September 6, 1928.[17]

By the beginning of 1930, Stout Air Lines had expanded the number of destinations it served by adding additional stops along its established routes. This resulted in the Michigan cities of Battle Creek and Kalamazoo along with South Bend, Indiana being added to the airline's service route connecting Detroit and Chicago. Meanwhile, expansion of the route between Detroit and Cleveland saw the inclusion of Toledo on the Michigan-Ohio border. Dictated by the distance traveled, one-way fares between various points on these routes ranged from $3 for the short Battle Creek-Kalamazoo flight to $28 for a trip between Cleveland and Chicago.[18]

In September of 1930, National Air Transport (N.A.T) purchased Stout Air Services. Both companies were divisions of the United Aircraft & Transport Corporation, with National engaged in carrying airmail and express freight between New York City, Chicago, and Dallas.[19] Commenting on the merger,

Lester D. Seymour, N.A.T. vice president and general manager, told reporters: "The various passenger services formerly operated by Stout will be continued and expanded. Combining as this does the oldest air passenger line organization and one of the oldest air mail operators, an unusually strong organization will result with which to operate both passenger and mail schedules over routes of the company."[20]

On November 19, 1930, the National Air Transport Service announced its intention of inaugurating the first direct all passenger air service between New York City and Chicago on December 1 of that year. This same route also provided service to Cleveland and Toledo.[21] Just six days later, N.A.T. revealed its plans to discontinue service between Detroit and Chicago and Detroit and Cleveland concurrent with the beginning of its previously announced direct service connecting New York with Chicago.[22] The end of Stout Air Lines came shortly thereafter when its stockholders voted to dissolve the company on December 24, 1930.[23]

Throughout its four years of operation, Stout Air Services carried more than 126,000 passengers over a distance in excess of 1,300,000 miles. Remarkably, the company managed to carry all these passengers to their destinations without injury—no small feat considering the dangers of air travel at the time. Although far overshadowed by the standards of today, the small pioneering steps taken by Stout Air Services, and many others, has led to a commercial aviation network that today connects every corner of the globe.

Chapter Four
A Simple Misunderstanding - 1905

Protruding from the northern shore of Michigan's Upper Peninsula, the Keweenaw Peninsula extends some sixty miles into the cold waters of Lake Superior. During the early 1840s, a geologist named Douglass Houghton discovered large copper deposits within this rugged landscape—a fact not unknown to prehistoric Native American tribes that first mined copper in this region approximately 3,000 years earlier. The news of Houghton's discovery sparked a copper boom that resulted in a large influx of laborers into that part of the state to mine the precious metal. While some of these mining operations failed miserably, others became highly successful, thereby allowing a lucky few to build enormous fortunes before the boom played itself out towards the end of the nineteenth century.

While termed as a peninsula, a series of interconnecting lakes, streams, and marshy areas actually separated the northernmost section of this landmass from its southern component. During the 1860s, the U.S. Federal Government and several mining interests combined forces to dredge out portions of this natural watercourse to form the Keweenaw Waterway (also known as the Portage Canal). Besides permitting ships to carry cargoes into and out of the copper rich area, the canal also gave captains piloting lake vessels the option of transiting between certain ports on Lake Superior without the necessity of taking the longer route around the northern tip of the Keweenaw Peninsula.

As the communities of Houghton and Hancock grew in size on the southern and northern sides of the Keweenaw Waterway respectively, it became apparent that the established ferry service would be unable to meet the future demands of commerce. As such, plans were developed in 1871 to build a 24-foot wide wooden bridge to connect the two northern Michigan communities. Although this project suffered a setback just a few years later as a casualty of a financial panic in 1873, it had gained enough momentum for construction to begin in the spring of 1875. Built with a rotating center section to allow the passage of ships, the wooden swing bridge soon rendered the local ferry service obsolete.

Twenty years later saw the construction of a new steel bridge when the old wooden structure had reached the end of its useful life. Incorporating two decks, the design of the new bridge allowed the movement of trains on its lower deck while pedestrians and streetcars traversed from one side of the waterway to the other on an upper deck. Opening in 1895, this bridge originally featured a wooden swing section that the Mineral Range Railroad Company replaced three years later with one built of steel.

On the afternoon of April 15, 1905, the steamer *Northern Wave* of the Mutual Transit Company was slowly making its way through the Keweenaw Waterway bound for the Quincy Smelter dock to load a cargo of copper ingots. Aboard the 312-foot steel package freighter, Captain Carringway requested the opening of the bridge spanning the canal by sounding his steam whistle.

From his post, bridge engineer Daniel Hardiman had no difficulty in hearing the bursts of sound emanating from the *Northern Wave*. Instead of hearing four blasts calling for him to open the bridge, however, Hardiman thought he only heard three. Believing the master of the approaching freighter had signaled the loading dock, the bridge operator took no immediate action.

Within a few moments, it became apparent to the confused

The Mutual Transit Company's steamer *Northern King* docked on the Keweenaw Waterway at Dollar Bay, Michigan. Belonging to the same fleet, this vessel was identical in design and appearance to the *Northern Wave*. (Library of Congress)

engineer that the onrushing ship was not going to stop. Realizing there was just seconds to avoid disaster, Hardiman made a frantic attempt to open the bridge. When the catches holding the span reacted very slowly to their operating wheel, however, his efforts were to prove futile. In spite of Hardiman enlisting the assistance of a nearby pedestrian in operating the bridge controls, it soon became obvious that a collision was unavoidable.[1]

It was at approximately 4:30 that spring afternoon when the bow of the *Northern Wave* smashed into the revolving bridge deck. Although the steamer had nearly come to a stop, its momentum was sufficient to smash the swing span into a pile of twisted wreckage. Pushed forcibly from its base, the demolished bridge span turned onto its side as it plummeted into the water below.

As the bridge experienced its busiest traffic hours between three and six o'clock in the afternoon, it is unsurprising that a number of people were traversing the structure at the time of the accident. Luckily, all of these individuals recognized the danger represented by the oncoming ship and successfully scrambled to safety before the collision.[2]

Besides Daniel Hardiman, only two other people, Robert Shields and Ralph DeMary, were present on the swing span when the *Northern Wave* reduced it to rubble. Both of these men were pedestrians, with the latter being employed by *The Mining Gazette*—the local newspaper. While Daniel Hardiman and Ralph DeMary received minor injuries when thrown against the steel structure of the collapsing bridge, Robert Shields managed to escape unharmed.[3] Although some early newspaper reports credit engineer Hardiman with saving a number of children on the bridge, subsequent accounts of the incident make no mention of such a heroic action.[4]

The cause of this accident stemmed from a misunderstanding between the bridge engineer and the master of the *Northern Wave* concerning the number of whistle blasts sounded by the steamer. Immediately following the collision, Captain Carringway blamed the bridge operator by claiming he acted properly when signaling for the bridge opening. For his part, Daniel Hardiman was adamant in his belief that the oncoming steamer only blew its whistle three times instead of the four that regulations required. Several people that witnessed the accident, however, corroborated the statements of the bridge engineer by reporting they only heard the *Northern Wave* sound its horn three times.[5]

With the only land connection across the Keweenaw Waterway severed, officials scrambled to formulate a response to minimize the economic impact of the accident. While the mangled remains of the bridge blocked the shipping channel, area docks remained accessible from either end of the canal. In this respect, the most severe consequence of the accident was the isolation of the northern section of the Keweenaw Peninsula, known locally as "Copper Island." Despite the level of destruction it dealt to the bridge span, the *Northern Wave* suffered only an estimated $500 worth of damage.[6]

Moving quickly, workers installed a temporary pontoon bridge across the gap opened by the steamer to allow the resumption of rail traffic through the area. Within three days of the accident, the two railroad companies that operated the bridge contracted the Wisconsin Bridge and Iron Company to remove the twisted wreckage from the canal. Working tirelessly, salvage crews managed to clear enough of the wrecked bridge to allow the resumption of navigation through the south opening on April 25, with the final removal of debris taking place just one month later. The recovery work also included the raising of a locomotive tender and a flatcar carrying a cargo of rails that had

A view of the shattered bridge deck and the pontoon barges placed in the opening to permit limited traffic across the canal. (Author's Collection)

fallen through the makeshift pontoon bridge on April 17, 1905.[7]

Consultations between the government and officials from the Copper Range Railroad resulted in the decision to build a new bridge rather than repair the damaged span. Awarded in July of that year, the contract for the new bridge stipulated the retention of the south pier while calling for the construction of a new center section and north pier. Meanwhile, the resumption of shipping had necessitated the removal of the temporary pontoon bridge. This resulted in establishment of a temporary carferry service to haul rail traffic between Houghton and Hancock beginning on April 24, 1905. Its construction taking somewhat longer than anticipated, the new span opened for traffic on April 8, 1906.[8]

Built by the Globe Iron Works at Cleveland, Ohio in 1889, the *Northern Wave* measured 312 feet 6 inches in length, 40 feet in beam, and had a depth of 24 feet 6 inches.[9] As such, this ship was one of six nearly identical steel package freighters built by Globe for the Northern Steamship Company.[10] Prior to its collision with the swing bridge connecting Houghton and Hancock, the *Northern Wave* was involved in at least one other incident on Lake Superior.

On October 2, 1901, the *Northern Wave* and the bulk carrier *Crescent City* came to the rescue of the wooden steamer *M. M. Drake* as it was sinking during a storm in eastern Lake Superior. The *Drake* was downbound on the lake towing the schooner-barge *Michigan*, when the captain of the barge signaled his craft was taking on water. As the steamer maneuvered to rescue the crew of the barge, a series of large waves led to a collision that resulted in both vessels heading to the bottom of Lake Superior. The *Northern Wave* and *Crescent City* managed to rescue all of the crewmembers belonging to two lost vessels with the exception of the barge's cook.[11]

During World War I, the federal government requisitioned a large number of lake freighters for ocean service. Now operated by the Great Lakes Transit Company, the *Northern Wave* was one such vessel. To enable the steamer to traverse the canal locks connecting the Great Lakes to the St. Lawrence River, it was cut in two by the American Ship Building Company at Buffalo, New York. After both sections arrived in Montreal, shipyard crews reassembled the *Northern Wave* in preparation for service on salt water.[12] Following the end of hostilities, this ship saw little service before being dismantled at Genoa, Italy in 1926.

Chapter Five
Captain Curtis Boughton – 1813-1896

The first shipment of peaches from St. Joseph consigned for delivery to Chicago on the opposite shore of Lake Michigan left that growing community in western Michigan during 1839 aboard the schooner *Henry U. King*. In command of the small wooden craft as it embarked upon its sixty-mile journey across the lake, Captain Curtis Boughton could have little idea that the cargo stowed aboard his vessel was to signify the beginning of the peach industry in the St. Joseph-Benton Harbor area. While most sources agree the enterprising shipmaster purchased the peaches from a number of small producers in Berrien County, it is probable that many came from a farm belonging to a prominent local businessman and future banker named Benjamin C. Hoyt.

Born in Bath, New York on September 13, 1813, Curtis Boughton's parents later moved to Cleveland, where they opened a tavern. Considering "13" a lucky number, he decided to run away from home at that age to become a cabin boy aboard vessels plying the Great Lakes. As was common in that era, Boughton eventually rose in rank to become a captain and acquire his own sailing vessels. Captain Boughton first arrived in St. Joseph during 1832 while serving as the master of a schooner trading between that city and Cleveland.[1]

This voyage must have made a lasting impression upon the young captain as he moved to Berrien County just two years later. Leaving his former home in Ohio behind, Curtis Boughton settled upon a piece of property on Niles Road just south of St.

35

Joseph.[2] In 1840, he married Katherine Miltibarger, with whom he would have three children. Of these, only two, James and John, or "Jim" and "Jack" as they were better known respectively, lived to see adulthood.[3]

With the arrival of the *Pioneer* in 1831, the citizens of St. Joseph witnessed their community's first visit by a steamboat. To place this event into perspective, it must be understood that steam powered vessels of the era represented the cutting edge of technology in much the same way as aircraft and spacecraft were to be looked upon by later generations. Although an infrequent caller to the small Michigan port, it was during one of these rare visits in July of 1834 that the *Pioneer* ran aground on a sandbar near the mouth of the St. Joseph River. At the mercy of the weather in this vulnerable position, a sudden gale tore the steamer to pieces a short time later. Using parts recovered from the wrecked *Pioneer*, Captain Boughton managed to build the schooner *Drift*, which he used to carry cargoes between St. Joseph and Chicago for a number of years afterwards.[4]

In addition to the *Drift*, Curtis Boughton subsequently acquired the schooners *Bancroft* and the *Henry U. King*, the latter of which he used to carry the pioneering peach shipment to Chicago. The *Bancroft* lasted until November of 1842 when it was lost during a fierce fall storm that ravaged the lower Great Lakes.[5] Wrecked at the mouth of the St. Joseph River—in the same general area that the *Pioneer* had met its end some eight years earlier—the entire crew of the *Bancroft* survived the accident through the heroic efforts of local villagers.[6]

Finding Chicago had an insatiable demand for peaches—some accounts indicate he may have received as much as $45 a barrel for the fuzzy-skinned fruit—Curtis Boughton followed his inaugural cross-lake trip to the growing metropolis with several additional shipments. The scale of this lucrative endeavor was limited, however, in direct proportion to the amount of peaches available.[7]   As a direct consequence, the fruit industry on the western shore of Michigan's Lower Peninsula grew significantly in the years following the opening of this trade route.

In 1849, Captain Boughton set about creating his own orchard when he planted 130 peach trees in St. Joseph, which began producing fruit three years later. Making a number of shipments to Chicago during the 1855 navigational season, Boughton received between 5 and 10 dollars per bushel for the peaches grown on his property.[8]

During his adult life, Captain Boughton involved himself in a number of business interests in the St. Joseph-Benton Harbor area. As such, he worked continuously to expand and improve the transportation of fruit from western Michigan to Chicago. It has been said that Boughton once turned down an offer to purchase several acres of land in what later became downtown Chicago for the paltry sum of five-hundred dollars.[9]

Throughout the years of the Civil War, Curtis Boughton demonstrated his charitable nature by using his private funds to help the families of soldiers serving in the war that had become destitute.[10]   Following the end of hostilities, the fruit industry along Michigan's west coast continued to grow as the nation grappled with the turbulent years of Reconstruction. By 1870, there were 600,000 peach trees in the area now occupied by modern day Benton Harbor and St. Joseph.[11]

For Captain Boughton, the years immediately following the war brought about several new business opportunities. Unfortunately, one of these endeavors would involve tragedy. Entering into a partnership with Allen Brunson and Captain John Morrison, Curtis Boughton became part owner of the steamer *Hippocampus*. Built in 1866 and given the name of a mythical seahorse, this propeller driven vessel measured 94 feet in length and 17 feet in beam.[12]

All went well for the *Hippocampus* until September 8, 1868

when it was lost after running into heavy weather on Lake Michigan midway between St. Joseph and Chicago. Operated by a crew of twenty-five, the small steamer was carrying sixteen passengers and a large cargo of peaches at the time of its loss. With most of the forty-one persons aboard the *Hippocampus* hailing from the St. Joseph-Benton Harbor area, a sense of shock descended upon the two small communities when initial reports indicated there were no survivors.

Although foggy conditions hampered the search on the day following the accident, good news arrived on September 11 when the tug *Minter* of Saugatuck docked at St. Joseph carrying fifteen survivors from the *Hippocampus*. Those lucky enough to survive the sinking had clung to a piece of the wrecked ship's upper works before the crew of the schooner *Trio* located them floating in the cold waters of the lake. The survivors consisted of nine crewmembers and six passengers. Among those rescued was the steamer's temporary master, Captain H. M. Brown, whom Captain John Morrison had hired for the trip after becoming ill.[13] The loss of the *Hippocampus* represents one of the worst disasters to occur on Lake Michigan during the mid-nineteenth century.

In May of 1869, Curtis Boughton became a director of the newly formed Michigan Lakeshore Railroad Company. The purpose of this firm was the construction of a railroad originating at New Buffalo in the extreme southwest corner of Berrien County near the Michigan-Indiana border and extending northward along the Lake Michigan shoreline. After connecting New Buffalo to St. Joseph in January of 1870, the railroad continued its expansion by reaching as far north as Muskegon and Big Rapids while also running a branch line between Holland and Grand Rapids. Completed in 1873 with a total of 246 miles of track laid, the company's original management abandoned the operation it to its bondholders the following year.

This arrangement lasted for about three years until its sale to Boston based interests after which it became the Chicago and West Michigan Railroad.[14]

Remaining active in both business and civic pursuits throughout the balance of his life, Captain Boughton served one term as Supervisor of St. Joseph Township in 1870. Over his professional career, Boughton came into ownership of several properties in and around St. Joseph-Benton Harbor area. Astute in several forms of commerce, he also entered into the profitable cross-lake movement of lumber and general goods from his hometown to Chicago and Milwaukee.[15] Curtis Boughton died on May 11, 1896, just one year following the passing of his wife. He is buried in the St. Joseph City Cemetery.

After reaching its peak during the late 1890s, the peach industry in western Michigan began a steady decline as it endured bouts with insects, disease, and the occasional early winter freeze. During this timeframe, the widespread introduction of refrigerated railcars allowed farmers in other states to ship their produce to Chicago, thus ending Michigan's stranglehold on its most important market. Although orchards in Michigan still produce upwards to 40 million pounds of peaches on an annual basis, these numbers are small in comparison to those generated by leading fruit producing states such as South Carolina and California. With its golden age now relegated to history, there is little doubt that Captain Boughton's pioneering shipment of peaches into Chicago during 1839 sparked the growth of one of the most important industries in western Michigan during the last half of the nineteenth century.

Chapter Six
Tragic Oversight – 1926

Despite the sun shining brightly in the clear blues above Southeastern Michigan on the afternoon of September 2, 1926, Willis Owen was having a bad day.[1] Employed by the Detroit, Monroe & Toledo Short Line Railway division of the Detroit United Lines, Owen had worked as both a conductor and motorman aboard his company's fleet of electrically powered interurban motor cars. Fulfilling the duties of motorman on this particular occasion, he was at the controls of car No. 7096 operating as train No. 224 on a regularly scheduled run between Detroit and Toledo. Suffering from a nagging toothache and having worked for over sixteen hours during the past twenty-four hour period, Owen eagerly awaited the end of his shift upon reaching the industrialized city located in the northwest corner of Ohio—a destination that also served as the motorman's home. Nearing Monroe as the car proceeded along its southward journey, Owen spotted his company's train No. 15 stopped on a siding at a location known along the route as Pine as it awaited No. 224's passage before resuming its northbound trip in the opposite direction. Forgetting that there should have been two trains stopped on the adjacent tracks, the fatigued motorman manipulated his controls to continue past the turnout that brought the route back to a single track. Passing that point, Owen continued toward the state line unaware that his mistake had placed train No. 224, and its passengers, on an irreversible path to disaster.

Incorporated on December 31, 1900, the Detroit United Railway

(DUR) was formed to consolidate the electric street railways in an around the city of Detroit. On March 1, 1906, this organization acquired the entire stock of the Detroit, Monroe & Toledo Short Line Railway Company. This transaction allowed the DUR (also known as the Detroit United Lines) to expand its network along the Michigan shoreline south of Detroit to the city of Toledo—a major manufacturing and shipping center located on the mouth of the Maumee River. In order of north to south, this route also served the cities of River Rouge, Ecorse, Wyandotte, Trenton, Gibraltar, Rockwood, Newport, Stony Creek, Monroe, and LaSalle.[2]

Capable of transporting small numbers of people over short distances not served by larger railroads, interurban railways became popular in many large population centers of the United States during the late 1800s and early 1900s. Powered by electricity, the motor car trolleys operating on these routes provided passengers with a clean and dependable method of transportation at a low cost. The year 1901, saw the completion of a new electric rail line connecting Toledo and Monroe. Operated by the Toledo & Monroe Railway, this 21 mile line was extended by an additional 35 miles just four years later to reach Detroit. With the completion of this project, the railway was renamed the Detroit, Monroe & Toledo Short Line Railway.[3]

As it was uneconomical to build two sets of tracks to separate the northbound and southbound traffic, the route contained several segments that featured only one set of tracks. To control the traffic over these sections, the railway company relied upon a timetable and train dispatch order system to avoid collisions. Under such an arrangement, trains traveling in opposite directions met at predetermined points on the route unless superseded by directions given by the dispatch department. The locations designated for the electrically powered cars to meet were equipped with sidings that allowed trains to stop while awaiting the passage of opposing traffic.

Having worked a ten-hour shift, Willis Owen left the Detroit, Monroe & Toledo Short Line Railway Company's yard in Toledo at 5:45 in the morning of September 1, 1926. After getting some breakfast, Owen went to a local dentist office seeking a remedy for a troublesome toothache. Arriving home at eleven o'clock, the motorman ate lunch before returning to duty just before two o'clock that afternoon without getting any rest. Following a nine -hour shift, Willis Owen finally went to bed at approximately 11:30 that evening after a long day made even more tiring by the throbbing pain emanating from his mouth.

Waking up at 5 a.m. the following morning, Owen returned to his job less than an hour later. Exhausted from working a heavy schedule over the past twenty-four hours, and unable to get much rest from the continuous pain of his toothache, Willis Owen was in no condition to be at the controls of a passenger carrying interurban motor car that September morning. With fifteen years of experience as both a conductor and motorman, however, he nonetheless performed his assigned duties throughout the morning hours without incident. By 12:45 that afternoon, car No. 7096, operating as train No. 224, departed the Oakwood station in Detroit to begin its southward journey toward Toledo. Accompanying Owen on this trip was Conductor Homer Adams, who had been with the company for 9 months and assigned to this particular run since the middle of August.[4]

Even as No. 224 was leaving Detroit, car No. 7529 with Motorman Andrew Schlegel and Conductor Charles Leatherman was already some twenty minutes outside of Toledo as it traveled northward as train No. 223. Running on regular schedules, the company's timetable dictated that these opposing trains were to meet at a point known as the Pine siding located just north of Monroe. This procedure called for the northbound

No. 223 to stop on the siding at that location to await the passage of No. 224 before continuing toward Detroit. Conversely, this same practice required the personnel aboard No. 224 to confirm they had passed No. 223 prior to proceeding past the southern turnout for Pine. Under this arrangement, both trains could safely reach their destinations without requiring any block-signal systems along the route—a procedure commonly used by interurban railways of the era.

Having traversed eighteen miles, Willis Owen brought No. 224 to a stop at Rockwood, where he and Conductor Adams received orders from the company's dispatch department to meet trains No. 221 and No. 15 at the Newport and Pine sidings respectively.[5] Both of these trains were running late that day and their inclusion into the queue of opposing traffic was in addition to other regularly scheduled trains on the route. With the new set of orders, Owen and Adams could now expect to meet both No. 15 and No. 223 at Pine, and it was, therefore, their

Although operated by the Lake Shore Electric Railway between Cleveland and Toledo, the interurban car shown in this photograph is very similar to the two involved in the collision just north of Monroe. (Author's Collection)

responsibility to verify these trains had stopped at that location before continuing toward their destination.

While operating on sections of the route upon which traffic flowed in both directions on the same set of tracks, a strict adherence to the rules established by the Detroit, Monroe & Toledo Short Line Railway was necessary to avoid collisions. Moving at relatively high speeds, the motor cars required a significant distance to stop despite being fitted with powerful airbrakes. With the electrically powered motor car's combination of a relatively high traveling speed and an inability to stop quickly in an emergency, their operators faced a daunting task that left little room for error.

Shortly after leaving the Rockwood station at 1:11 that fateful afternoon, the crew of No. 224 spotted train No. 221 stopped at the Newport siding as they continued toward Toledo. When the next meeting point at Pine came into view, Willis Owen saw a single motor car halted on the siding awaiting his car's passage. Although sighting the operator of the stationary vehicle, Owen failed to get its identifying number and was therefore unable to establish it as being train No. 223 or the behind schedule No. 15. It was at this precise moment that the fatigued motorman did a very human thing—he simply forgot that his updated orders and standard timetable schedule dictated that there should have been two trains at the Pine siding. Perhaps distracted by something or someone in the passenger compartment, Conductor Adams compounded his fellow crewman's critical oversight by also forgetting about meeting a second train at the siding.[6] Unaware of his error, Willis Owen continued past the solitary interurban car at Pine and onto the single-track section leading into Monroe. By doing so, he placed train No. 224 and all of its occupants on an unavoidable collision course with the northbound No. 223.

About two miles north of Monroe, the route established by the Detroit, Monroe & Toledo Short Line Railway required southbound traffic to negotiate a left curve measuring approximately ¼ mile in length. While the terrain in this area is flat, the trees and overhead power line poles bordering the railway's right of way limited visibility along this stretch of track to no more than 1,000 feet.[7]

Entering into this curve at 45 mph, Willis Owen struggled to see around the sharp bend as the surrounding countryside rushed by. Peering through the window of his duty station, the motorman was horrified to spot another car heading right for him on the tracks ahead. With only seconds to spare, Owen did what he could to minimize the impending collision by slamming his car's motors into reverse and engaging the emergency brakes. At the same time, he also activated the motor car's sanding equipment to maximize the friction between its wheels and the steel rails. Performing his duties in another part of the car, Homer Adams first became aware of the emergency when the motorman began his desperate effort to slow the car. Quickly working his way forward, the conductor first sighted the onrushing train No. 223 when it was barely 300 feet away.[8]

Pushing their way north at 45 mph, the crew of No. 223 had no reason to expect anything out of the ordinary as they prepared to meet the southbound No. 224 at the Pine siding. While traversing over the curve north of Monroe, however, the routine nature of Motorman Andrew Schlegel's afternoon took an ominous turn when he saw an oncoming train suddenly materialize just 700 feet away. With the motormen of both cars sighting each other at nearly the same moment, the braking actions taken by the two men took place nearly simultaneously. Despite these desperate efforts, the estimated 90 mph initial closure rate between the two cars translated into little more than 7 seconds of warning time, thereby making a collision unavoidable.

Filled with passengers, both cars slammed head-on in a

spectacular collision at 1:24 that afternoon at a point approximately 1 ¾ miles north of Monroe. The impact forced car No. 7096 of train No. 224 from the tracks and onto the forward half of its northbound counterpart. Although the entangled remains of the two cars remained upright in a mass of twisted wreckage, both suffered heavy damages in the collision. Car No. 7096, from which Motorman Willis leapt just moments before the accident, had the first six feet of its structure demolished, while nearly nineteen feet of car No. 7529 of train No. 223 was reduced to little more than a pile of bent steel, broken glass, and splintered wood.

Unfortunately, the level of devastation resulting from the collision was not limited solely to material damages as it also left eight people dead and another twenty-six injured. The fatalities included seven that died at the scene and one man that passed away a short time later at a hospital in nearby Monroe.[9] Those killed from Michigan included Elizabeth Burns of Blissfield; Joseph Rosenthal of Dundee, A. W. Hebner and Ben Fitch of Detroit, and Dr. Charles T. Southworth of Monroe. Others to lose their lives that afternoon included Jack Ferguson and Jacob Huber of Toledo, and W. E. Rooney of Sandwich, Ontario.

Upon learning of the accident, every available physician from the Monroe area descended upon the scene to offer medical assistance to those pulled alive from the wrecked cars. While several of those aboard the two trains managed to survive the accident with little more than minor cuts and bruises, at least ten others were hospitalized at Monroe with serious injuries. Having leapt from train No. 224 just moments before it slammed into the opposing northbound train, Motorman Owen required only minor treatment for superficial injuries before returning to his home in Toledo.[10] While the crash also injured Conductor Adams, he managed to make a prompt recovery and was able to provide investigators with many details concerning the events leading up to the accident.

While the crew of train No. 224 managed to survive the collision with relatively minor injuries, their counterparts aboard No. 223 were not as fortunate. Having suffered nearly fatal injuries, rescuers rushed Motorman Andrew Schlegel and Conductor Charles Leatherman to the hospital in Monroe. In addition, a student motorman named Arthur Heffner accompanying the crew of No. 223 on that fateful day as part of his training died shortly after the accident. His death, along with that of George Hertel of New York on September 3, 1926 brought the final death toll of the collision to ten.[11]

Immediately following the accident, the Interstate Commerce Commission began an investigation into the circumstances leading up to the collision. While being questioned by investigators, Motorman Willis Owen of the southbound train No. 224 admitted he had forgotten about the northbound train No. 223 due to the confusion of receiving the last minute orders to meet the late northbound trains at locations other than their normal meeting points. In addition, Owen also told of his personal judgment on the afternoon in question being adversely affected by a persistent toothache and fatigue from having been on duty for several hours over the previous two days. Conductor Homer Adams corroborated the motorman's testimony by admitting he also forgot about meeting train No. 223 while observing the halted No. 15 at the Pinc siding. Furthermore, he told of not noticing anything unusual in the behavior or actions of Motorman Owen during the time leading up to the crash.[12]

Throughout their inquiry, investigators found their efforts complicated by the medical condition of the two surviving crewmembers of train No. 223. Although released from the hospital one month following the accident, the lingering effects of Motorman Schlegel's injuries precluded him from enduring an extensive period of questioning by officials. Despite this, however, the motorman did tell of his train moving at approximately 45 mph when he first noticed the oncoming train No. 224 at a distance of 700 feet. Although testifying the brakes were in good condition, Schlegel could provide no estimation as to how fast his motor car was moving at the time of the collision. Having suffered a fractured skull and other serious injuries, doctors released Charles Leatherman from the hospital on October 7, 1926. Returning to his home at Oakwood, the conductor's injuries prevented him from providing any statements to the Interstate Commerce Commission.[13]

In his statements to investigators, Willis Owen told of slowing his train from its original 45 mph speed to an estimated 15 mph when the accident occurred. Although the Interstate Commerce Commission failed to establish the precise speed at which No. 223 was moving at the time of impact, it is reasonable to assume that Schlegel's braking action had slowed the motor car to about half of its initial 45 mph speed at the point of collision. With these values, it is possible to make a simple estimation that the two trains came together at an approximate speed of 55 feet per second or 37 ½ mph. With each of the motor cars weighing around 60,000 pounds apiece, it is remarkable that the death toll from the accident did not reach an even greater magnitude.

When the Interstate Commerce Commission issued its final report on this accident on October 9, 1926, it laid the blame for the collision squarely upon Motorman Owen and Conductor Adams of train No. 224. Regardless of this conclusion, the investigation also found that Willis Owen had been on duty for 16 hours during the 24 hours leading up to the collision—a clear violation of federal law. Compounded by a lack of rest and the persistent tooth ailment, this fact led investigators to conclude that Owen was in a depressed and nervous state when the accident took place. While partially absolving Motorman Owen of guilt in the accident, the Interstate Commerce Commission found no reason for Conductor Adams to become confused as to meeting a regularly scheduled train operating on an established timetable in addition to receiving orders to meet a late northbound train at the Pine siding. Although finding fault with the number of hours worked by Willis Owen, the investigation found no other employees of the Detroit, Monroe & Toledo Short Line Railway involved in this accident as being in violation of the federal service law.[14]

By the time of the accident described in this chapter, the interurban railway system in the United States was entering a dark period in its history. Facing stiff competition from the automobile and improved highways, these operations suffered a steady decline in passenger traffic beginning during the mid-1920s. Unable to survive the dramatic drop in revenue, most interurban railways went out of business by the middle of the following decade. In recent years, many have questioned the wisdom of abandoning these high-speed routes that served large metropolitan areas.

Chapter Seven
Alpena's Great Fire of 1872

In the fall of 1856, a group of five men consisting of George N. Fletcher, James K. Lockwood, John S. Minor, John Oldfield, and a surveyor named E. A. Breakenridge landed on Thunder Bay Island in northern Lake Huron. There, they met Daniel Carter, whom had previously traveled to the area to act as George Fletcher's agent in acquiring lands.[1] Located at the entrance to Thunder Bay some 160 sailing miles north of Port Huron, the elongated island is home to one of the earliest lighthouses constructed in Michigan. Carter had arrived on Thunder Bay Island to arrange passage on a downbound steamer in order to retrieve his family from St. Clair. Instead of continuing his journey, however, Carter accompanied the party off the island and to a small clearing located at the mouth of the Thunder Bay River that would one day become the city Alpena.

With the Civil War just five years in the future, the 1856 presidential election reflected the increasing political divide within the nation concerning the issue of slavery. As staunch Republicans, Fletcher, Lockwood, and Breakenridge had resolved to give the settlement they were about to establish the name of Fremont, in honor of John C. Fremont—the first presidential candidate named by the Republican Party and its candidate in that year's election. To this end, they had brought a Fremont election flag on their trip north. Of the remaining men, Daniel Carter was a loyal Democrat, while John Minor and John Oldfield—both Canadians—held neutral political views.

Shortly after landing at the mouth of the Thunder Bay River, the men located and cut a large cedar log upon which they nailed the Fremont flag. As Daniel Carter looked on, the other members of the group—perhaps in a somewhat inebriated state—made several futile attempts to raise the flag above their newly named outpost. When asked to lend a hand, Carter remained steadfast in his political beliefs by replying he "would not help raise a flag that he would not support."[2] Undeterred, the men continued their efforts, which, after several further attempts, resulted in the Fremont flag flying proudly above their heads.[3]

Mostly through the efforts of local business owners and James K. Lockwood, the Michigan Legislature passed an act on February 14, 1857 establishing Alpena County and naming Fremont as county seat.[4] Two years later, the legislature approved a petition put forth by several citizens of Fremont—many of which were Democrats—to rename their community the village of Alpena.[5]

Bordered by dense pine forests, it was only natural that Alpena became one of Michigan's busiest lumber centers during the mid -1800s. Beginning in 1864, the village experienced a period of substantial growth with the construction of several new sawmills. With the mills came workers and their families, along with merchants, hotel operators, churches, and the need for public buildings. This influx of people resulted in the village's population growing from only 674 inhabitants in 1864 to 2,756 just six years later.[6] On March 29, 1871, a little more than fourteen years since the Fremont election flag first fluttered in the skies above the mouth of the Thunder Bay River, the state legislature granted Alpena a city charter.

Despite the prosperity of the local economy, however, Alpena still lacked any financial institutions. As such, all of the businesses operating in the area conducted their banking activities at Detroit. Consequently, a large proportion of the money paid out by these firms was spent in that city, which had the effect of stifling trade in Alpena. This situation ended in the spring of 1872 when the Alpena Banking Co. and The Exchange Bank opened for business.[7]

Like many other Michigan lumber towns, Alpena was no stranger to fire. While many of these blazes resulted in the damage or loss of a single structure, others were of a much greater magnitude. One such example took place on April 9, 1871, when a fire destroyed many buildings in the growing city, among which included the Star Hotel, Huron House, and Evergreen Hall. Many of those that suffered losses in the blaze were either uninsured or had policies that covered only the debt carried on their property. Therefore, some business owners found themselves without financial resources to recover from the conflagration.[8]

As this incident took place immediately following Alpena's incorporation as city, one of the first official acts of the new city government was the establishment of a fire company and the acquisition of a steam fire engine. In May of 1871, the city council passed an ordinance organizing a fire department, while at same time electing Albert L. Power as foreman of the sixty-three person strong fire company. By the time of that year's Fourth of July celebration, the formation of the fire department had progressed far enough along to allow the men involved to proudly march through the city streets in full dress uniform alongside their newly acquired steam fire engine. To honor a local Indian chief, officials gave both the fire brigade and its engine the name Sog-on-e-qua-do, or "Thunder Cloud."[9]

Shortly after losing the Huron House in the April 1871 fire, Samuel Boggs purchased a piece of property on Second Street, upon which he built a hotel named the Sherman House. It was in a barn behind this structure that fire erupted at approximately

4:45 in the afternoon of Friday, July 12, 1872. Although the fire department arrived on scene within minutes of the alarm, the fire spread quickly as it consumed the hay stored in the barn. Within minutes, the Sherman House and Goodrich's Jewelry Store were also ablaze. Fanned by a northwest wind, the fire quickly outpaced the best efforts of the outmatched firefighters and had soon reached the row of buildings on the opposite side of the street.[10]

Within minutes of reaching the south side of Second Street, the conflagration had laid waste to the buildings in that block, among which included the Burrell House and the Huron House. It was not until six o'clock that evening that the fire was contained, by which time it had consumed some three and one-half blocks of the downtown area containing approximately sixty -five buildings.[11] The devastation brought about by the fire was not limited to property losses as four people perished in the inferno while many others were injured. Among those killed was Mrs. Westbrook, the proprietor of a millinery store, who was unable to escape the fast moving flames and burned to death in the street outside her establishment. Seeing his mother in peril, George Westbrook attempted to save her but suffered such serious burns that he died the following day. Picking through the smoldering debris, searchers also located the remains of two other men that did not survive what locals came to refer to in the upcoming years as the Great Fire.[12]

In addition to the buildings previously mentioned, the fire also destroyed the Eagle Hotel, Union Hotel, A. Auspach's Dry Goods Store, A. Herr's Furniture Store, A. L. Power & Co. Grocery Store, C. C. Whitney's Drug Store, Dow & Goodnow's store, and the Potter Bros. Hardware Store. Also lost in the fire was the County Clerk's Office, Mayor Albert Pack's residence and office, along with several boarding houses and private homes. As the list of demolished structures demonstrates, the fire was especially devastating to the city's lodging establishments.[13]

Despite the destruction of the County Clerk's Office, the county records survived intact. Remarkably, some of these documents had encountered one previous brush with fire. Having entered into an agreement with the Alpena County Board of Supervisors in 1863, Samuel E. Hitchcock built a courthouse at the intersection of Chisholm and Washington streets. Seven years later, a fire believed—but never proven—to be the work of an arsonist destroyed the courthouse along with many of the records stored there. Following the blaze, officials had the court offices and surviving papers moved to rooms above the Potter Brothers Hardware Store on Second Street. These documents included county records of marriages, deaths, naturalization, tax assessments, court proceedings, and account books.[14] When the fire of July 12, 1872 erupted, some quick action on the part of those involved resulted in the records safe removal before the burning of the offices.

The fiery disaster caused at least $180,000 in damages, of which insurance covered approximately $70,000.[15] This left many of those affected without money to rebuild—a circumstance in common with previous fires to afflict the Alpena area and a risk taken by anyone engaging in commerce or living in a lumber town of the era. Despite the financial and material cost of the fire, the lifeblood of Alpena's economic prosperity—its numerous lumber mills—remained untouched, thus allowing the community to rebound within a short period of time.

Among the many businesses that suffered heavily from this event was the *Alpena Weekly Argus* newspaper, which lost its offices in the fire. Only partially insured like many other firms affected by this disaster, the *Argus* carried no coverage on its stock. The owners of the newspaper proved resilient, however, and within forty-five days of the fire, the *Alpena Weekly Argus* resumed operation after acquiring new printing equipment.[16]

While no definitive cause for the fire was ever established, some belief existed that its origin lay in a whiskey dispute. To this end, officials assigned a detective to investigate the matter. Although this inquiry led to a number of arrests, the resulting trials failed to prove any of the allegations leveled against the men charged.[17]

In the aftermath of the July 12, 1872 fire, the city government passed a new ordinance establishing a fire limit by stipulating the construction of new buildings in the disaster area be of brick rather than wood—a measure futilely opposed by many as being unnecessary.[18] The incident also made it apparent that the size of Alpena's fire department was insufficient to battle a blaze of such magnitude. This was one of the factors that influenced the city council's July 1875 decision to approve the purchase of a Silsby No. 4 rotary steam fire engine along with a hose cart and associated equipment for a sum $5,850.[19]

Within a few months, several new brick buildings began replacing the burnt out wooden structures as life slowly returned to normal in Alpena. Fire remained a constant threat to the citizens of the Northern Michigan community throughout the balance of the nineteenth century, instances of which on some occasions proved quite disastrous. One of the worst occurred nearly sixteen years to the day of the 1872 fire, when a blaze destroyed fourteen blocks in the city's Third Ward on July 11, 1888. Burning some two-hundred buildings and inflicting an estimated $400,000 in property losses, the fire left at least 3 people dead and another 1,300 homeless.[20]

Chapter Eight
The Balkan Mine Disaster - 1914

In 1846, William A. Burt, a federal land surveyor and inventor of the forerunner to the modern typewriter, found evidence of iron ore deposits near Crystal Falls in the lower western half of Michigan's Upper Peninsula. Three years later, a federal geologist named J. W. Foster reported finding sizable beds of ore during a survey conducted along the Menominee River. In 1851, some five years after Burt's initial report, Foster along with fellow geologist J. D. Whitney confirmed the presence of iron ore in the Crystal Falls area of the Western Menominee Range.

The iron ranges of upper Michigan, along with those in Wisconsin and Minnesota, were to play a major role in the growth of the domestic steel industry during the late 1800s. From these ranges, miners extracted thousands of tons of ore to feed the hungry blast furnaces that provided a young nation with the steel it needed to grow into a world power. Benefiting from their close proximity to the waters of the upper Great Lakes, the location of these deposits allowed the heavy ore to be loaded aboard lake freighters that provided a highly efficient transportation method to supply the busy mills located in the states bordering the lower lakes.

Although financial constraints following the Panic of 1873 slowed initial plans to develop the Menominee Iron Range, economic conditions had recovered sufficiently by 1877 that the Breen and Vulcan mines recorded shipments that year totaling just over 10,000 tons of ore. Within two years, the explosive growth of the mining industry on the range resulted in the annual receipts of ore shipments reaching 200,000 tons. Within six years, the mines working the Menominee Range had reached a significant milestone by surpassing the one million ton mark in combined annual ore shipments.[1]

In 1881, John M. Longyear, a developer with extensive mining interests in the Michigan's Upper Peninsula, located an outcrop of iron in a swampy area south of Crystal Falls. This discovery led to Edward N. Breitung forming the Mastodon Iron Company, which shipped its first ore the following year. Shuttered by its owners following the Panic of 1893, the mine remained idle until its acquisition by the Balkan Mining Company in 1913. Formed by the Picklands Mather & Co., this firm went to work developing the long idled property along with the nearby Balkan and Judson mines.[2]

Located near the village of Alpha in Iron County, the Balkan Mine was approximately fifteen miles east of Iron River, which is about half that many miles north of the Michigan-Wisconsin border. Founded in 1910, Alpha owed its existence to the mining industry—a trait in common with many communities in the northwestern Michigan county. In anticipation of upcoming plans to develop the mines near the small settlement during 1914, the Chicago based Mining World Company's publication *Mining and Engineering World* dated February 7 of that year contained the following report:

> At the east side of Iron County, a summer of exceptional building activity is in store for the new town of Alpha. The Longyear interests are here developing the Judson mine and Picklands, Mather & Co. the Balkan. Both of these properties will eventually rank with the very largest producers on the Menominee range.

Involving both open-pit and underground mining methods, the extraction of iron ore from the Balkan Mine created a series of

large cuts in the surface of the land.[3]   Water accumulation is a
constant problem facing those engaged in mining operations. On
the night of Tuesday, July 14, 1914, a crew of twelve men
ventured down a shaft some five-hundred feet deep that had
been drilled north of the mine's open cut. Working in a drift
extending from this shaft, the men began drilling into the roof
above their heads as they attempted to remove a deposit of water
and allow the mine to dry. As the drill worked its way through a
layer of iron, however, a tremendous force suddenly forced it
back out of the hole. Almost instantly, a steady stream of
quicksand exploded from the newly opened borehole and onto
the men below. Immediately recognizing the precariousness of
their situation, the miners began a desperate dash for the shaft
located approximately 300 feet away.[4]

Within moments of the first burst of quicksand, the roof
collapsed as a raise approximately sixty feet in height gave way.[5]
Exhibiting a vigor only nature could produce, the watery mass
sought to fill every open space of the mine. Catching up with the
fleeing men, the wall of quicksand buried seven of the miners
that did not reach the exit in time. Of the men lucky enough to
reach the ladder leading to the surface, one barely survived after
becoming buried up to his shoulders within the muddy morass
just feet away from safety.[6] Pulling himself up the ladder, this
individual escaped only after leaving his boots and clothes
behind in the quicksand. Although exiting naked from the shaft,
this man was fortunate beyond measure by narrowly escaping
the unsympathetic clutches of death.[7]

Ranging between the ages of 22 and 45 years in age,
contemporary accounts of this accident report all of the men
killed in the mine as "foreigners." The youngest of these was
Victor Pallaora, while Dimitar Radaovitch represented the most
elderly person to lose his life that day. Other victims included
Batista Battan, Dominco Bevola, Antonio Boschi, Jacob Maki, and

Batesta Rossi. With the exception of Dimitar Radaovitch and Batista Battan, all of these men were unmarried.[8]

Carried in newspapers across the nation, the initial press reports coming out of Alpha, Michigan concerning the deaths of the miners made no secret about the difficulty in recovering their bodies by predicting this process to take weeks or several months.[9]

Perhaps competing for space with accounts concerning the beginning of the First World War, little more mention of this tragedy appeared within the pages of regional newspapers throughout the following months. One exception, however, took place three weeks after the accident when the *Escanaba Morning Press* reported that crews had recovered the body of Antonio Boschi on July 25, 1914.[10] Finding his remains just a few feet away from the shaft leading to safety, searchers theorized that the man's heavy rubber boats slowed his progress to such an extent that he could not escape the onrushing quicksand. To illustrate the enormity of the task facing those involved with the recovery operation, the newspaper closed its report with the following statement: "Work is being pushed right along towards recovering the bodies and if they are not all taken out soon it will be no fault of the Balkan people."

Far overshadowed by reports of the carnage visited upon the battlefields of Europe during the early months of the twentieth century's first global war, history remains mute as to whether or not searchers ever located the remaining six bodies entombed within the mineshaft. Following the loss of the seven men, the Balkan Mine went on to provide a steady stream of iron ore over a production period that lasted for another twenty years.[11]

Chapter Nine
Cholera Epidemic at Detroit - 1832

In April of 1832, a group of 1,500 Indians under the leadership of a Sauk warrior named Black Hawk crossed the Mississippi River from Iowa and into Illinois. The federal government responded by dispatching the U.S. Army to join the state militias mobilized to meet this threat. Although composed primarily of men from Illinois, the militia force also included contingents from Indiana, Missouri, and the Michigan Territory. Known as the Black Hawk War, the engagements of the resulting conflict took place in Illinois and the portion of the Michigan Territory that later became the state of Wisconsin. The movement of federal forces into this area of operations benefited greatly from the waterways of the Great Lakes that permitted the government to deploy its forces into the Chicago area with minimal difficulty.

The year 1832 also saw the onset of a cholera pandemic throughout much of Europe and North America. In the United States, no community suffered more heavily from the disease outbreak than New York City. With an eventual death toll reaching at least 3,500, it is unsurprising that a panic set in amongst the city's some 250,000 citizens—half of which fled their homes for the perceived safety of the surrounding countryside. As one of the world's most easily communicable diseases, the cholera outbreak quickly made its way up the Hudson River to spread through the communities bordering the Erie Canal connecting Albany with Buffalo on Lake Erie.

On July 4, 1832, the steamer *Henry Clay* arrived at Detroit carrying 370 soldiers destined for fighting in the Black Hawk

War. When one of the soldiers belonging to this detachment died the following day from cholera, the military authorities ordered the *Clay* to Hog Island (later Belle Isle). A short time later, the paddle wheel steamer resumed its journey to Chicago by steaming northward through Lake St. Clair and into the St. Clair River. During this time, however, cholera had spread to so many of the men aboard the *Henry Clay* that it became necessary to stop at Fort Gratiot near the entrance to Lake Huron.[1]

After having the sick removed from the ship to receive treatment at an impromptu hospital established at the military outpost, the commander in charge of the operation ordered those capable of walking to make their way south to Detroit. During the arduous sixty-mile trek through the wilderness, several of these men died after becoming sick or falling victim to other perils along the trail. All told, approximately 150 of those making the trip managed to reach Detroit on July 8, 1832. Departing a short time later aboard the steamer *William Penn*, several of these soldiers also contracted cholera. This resulted in the decision to land the men ashore just southwest of Detroit, where they established a camp in Springwells Township until the epidemic subsided.[2] The combination of cholera and the desertions caused by fears of catching the disease, resulted in nearly half of the soldiers not reaching their intended destination to participate in the Black Hawk War.[3]

Even as the soldiers were making their way south from Fort Gratiot, cholera was beginning to make its presence known at Detroit. After two people died of the disease on July 6, a panic set in amongst the community's 3,600 inhabitants that led to many people closing their businesses and fleeing the city. Concerns of cholera spreading to the surrounding towns prompted many of these communities to enforce a strict quarantine against the citizens of Detroit. Among others, these measures included armed guards patrolling the roads leading into Pontiac with instructions to turn back anyone found to be fleeing the stricken city. The dangerous combination of fear and firearms resulted in a number of violent incidents breaking out between the opposing parties. One such instance took place when the driver of a mail coach refused to stop at Ypsilanti so a local health inspector could examine his passengers. Panicked by the driver's actions, the nearby guards opened fire at the coach and killed one of its horses. The hysteria gripping the area also led to the razing of bridges leading into Rochester and the forcible eviction of people from Detroit out of local hotels.[4]

Meanwhile, the citizens of Detroit took it upon themselves to provide what assistance they could offer to those stricken with the disease. Among those responding to the crisis, was Col. Andrew Mack, the U.S. collector for the city's port and owner of the Mansion House Hotel, who provided shelter to many of the some 200 people that contracted cholera between July and September of that year. Perhaps the most devoted effort toward caring for the sick and burying the dead, however, came from Father Gabriel Richard, the Catholic priest of the Ste. Anne Church.

Born in Saintes, France on October 15, 1767 Gabriel Richard studied at the village school and later at the theological seminary at Angers before receiving his priesthood at Paris in 1788. During the French Revolution, a law went into effect that compelled all priests to take an oath of allegiance to the new government. When Father Richard refused, he joined the many Catholic priests forced to leave that country. Crossing the Atlantic, he reached Baltimore on June 24, 1792 after which he engaged in providing religious work in the lands west of the Mississippi River that later became part of the Louisiana Purchase. Working at a number of the small missions in this region, Gabriel Richard received instructions on March 2, 1798 directing him to Detroit, where he arrived in June of that year in

This 1820 view of Detroit depicts the arrival of the *Walk-in-the-Water*, the first steamboat to ply the upper Great Lakes. (Library of Congress)

the company of a fellow missionary named John Dilhet. Following their arrival, both men went to work assisting the Reverend Michel Lavadoux at the Ste. Anne Church.[5]

Having spent 1799 traveling throughout northern Michigan, Gabriel Richard returned to Detroit in October of that year to oversee the reconstruction of the Ste. Anne Church to accommodate the growing number of parishioners. Just a few years after this $3,000 project was completed, a fire swept through Detroit on June 11, 1805 that destroyed most of the buildings in the city, including the Ste. Anne Church. With a dispute over the location to build another church delaying its construction for several years, Father Richard began performing religious services from a tent before moving them to a warehouse and later onto a rented farm. Fueled by a proposal to remove the cemetery from the old church grounds, the disagreement concerning the location of erecting a new church was not resolved until Bishop Benedict Flaget arrived in 1818 to negotiate a settlement. Prior to this, the British briefly

63

imprisoned Gabriel Richard at Sandwich, Ontario during the War of 1812 when he refused to swear an allegiance to Britain. Besides his service as a Catholic priest, Father Richard also served a single term in the U.S. House of Representatives during 1823-25 as a delegate from the Michigan Territory.[6]

When Detroit's first cholera epidemic occurred, sixty-four year old Gabriel Richard rose to the challenge of providing medical care and spiritual guidance to those stricken with the disease. Working tirelessly through the crisis, he eventually contracted cholera himself and died at three o'clock in the morning of September 13, 1832 just as the outbreak was entering its final days. Felt deeply within the growing community, Father Richard's death brought about a universal outpouring of sympathy from both the Protestant and Catholic mourners attending his funeral later that same day. During this ceremony, the remains of Gabriel Richard were laid to rest in a crypt beneath the Ste. Anne Church. Later, church officials installed a memorial window depicting the fallen priest at a prominent location just inside its entrance.[7]

By late July, the cholera epidemic had abated sufficiently to allow business to return to normal in the city.[8] When it finally burned itself out two months later, the disease had left at least ninety-six dead in its wake—a mortality rate approaching fifty-percent.

Enduring three additional cholera epidemics that resulted in significant death tolls over the next twenty-two years, the 1832 outbreak was in no way the only such calamity to visit Detroit during this part of its history. In 1834, an epidemic stretching between August and September of that year left an estimated 700 dead, this being followed fifteen years later by an even more grievous return of cholera that killed 1,200 persons. In its last major brush with the disease, Detroit experienced another outbreak in 1854 that proved fatal to over 200 of its citizens.[9]

These instances of cholera took place during a period in which Detroit experienced an explosive growth in population as more settlers moved into the Midwestern United States. Between 1830 and 1840, the city's population had risen from 2,200 to 9,100 residents. More than doubling to 21,000 over the next decade, the continuous influx of people saw Detroit grow to have just over 45,000 inhabitants in 1860. Despite experiencing additional cholera scares throughout the balance of the nineteenth century, the rapidly growing city—primarily through preventive sanitation measures—managed to avoid any serious outbreaks of the disease following the 1854 visitation.

Chapter Ten
Dog Sled Teams of the Upper Peninsula

Michigan's admission into the Union in 1837 came at a time in which many of its residents lived in communities spread across the most isolated areas of the state. This was particularly true in the northern reaches of the Lower Peninsula and the then largely unexplored Upper Peninsula—the western portion of which the federal government ceded to Michigan to resolve a dispute with Ohio concerning the Toledo Strip. Due to its geography, the majority of the earliest settlements in the state sprung up along waterways that provided both a dependable source of fresh water and an efficient method to move people and goods.

The annual onset of winter, however, brought frigid temperatures that froze the rivers and lakes solid, thereby closing them to further navigation until the arrival of the spring thaw. In Michigan's northern region, this period usually lasted from about late November and mid-April of the following year. As such, the arrival of the first ship in spring was an eagerly anticipated event that sharply contrasted with the less cheerful departure of the final ship in late autumn.

During the early to mid-1800s, communities such as Sault Ste. Marie and Marquette in the Upper Peninsula were barely more than frontier towns that were isolated from the outside world for approximately five months of the year. The far-flung nature of Michigan's most northern territory prompted Henry Clay, a prominent nineteenth century senator from Kentucky, to state his opposition to the building of a shipping canal at Sault Ste. Marie in 1840 by boldly proclaiming it, "a work beyond the remotest settlement in the United States, if not in the moon."[1] In the days before railroads and roads reached the far corners of the state, many remote settlements depended primarily upon dog sled teams for the delivery of mail and other vital supplies during the harsh winter months.

Although more commonly associated with Alaska when most people think in terms of American history, the use of dog sled teams played a significant role in the development of Michigan's more remote regions throughout the 1800s and well into the early years of the twentieth century. Not only did the men operating the dog teams transport supplies to these outlying areas, they also provided a link to the civilized world by bringing with them the latest news. In fact, many points in the Upper Peninsula were only accessible by water during the summer and dog sledges in the winter.

Tasked with moving the mail year-round, the U.S. Post Office Department relied heavily upon dog teams to reach these areas during Michigan's coldest season. Able to operate when heavy snow and thick ice prohibited all other forms of cross-country travel, the longest route established by this service was the bi-weekly run between Saginaw and Marquette. Many of the men employed by the postal service were Native Americans. With it being unsafe to traverse the heavy woods in many areas, the drivers often had to follow the shoreline and pass over ice to reach their destinations.   Consequently, the trip between Saginaw and Marquette could involve a journey of between six and seven hundred miles through the wilderness.[2]

Owned by the government, the wooden sledges used by the mail carriers measured approximately ten feet long and fourteen inches wide. They also had smooth undersides due to the lack of runners. While parcels of mail wrapped in watertight material were the primary cargo of this operation, the government did not prevent the couriers from carrying other items for private profit as the need arose. To address the obvious dangers presented by an arduous trek through the wilderness, postal officials adopted the policy of dispatching the sledges in pairs. Pulled by a team of four dogs, two couriers accompanied each of the mail sleds. While one of the men ran in front of the toboggan like sleigh, the other followed behind to keep it upright while passing over uneven terrain with the help of a long pole extending upwards from the rear of its wooden frame.

The positioning of the dogs was extremely critical in assuring the endeavor's overall success. Using their hard-earned experience, the men harnessed their best-trained dog at the front to act as leader. Of equal importance, they also placed the dog deemed most capable of preventing the sledge from tipping at the rear of the team. In this arrangement, a good dog team could cover between forty and sixty miles per day. Traveling throughout the hours of daylight, the men bedded down for the night alongside their animals under the cover of pine trees or alongside a snow bank offering protection from the wind. After the dogs had traversed a particular route once, the men could rely upon them to find their way by instinct during times of uncertainty. For all their hard work, the dogs received a daily ration of cornmeal mixed with tallow.[3]

Almost equal in distance to the Marquette run was the mail route between Saginaw and Sault Ste. Marie. Among the men engaged on this route were John Boucher and Antoine Paquette, both of whom were natives of Sault Ste. Marie—a community commonly referred to as the "Soo."[4] For a quarter of a century, these two men made the arduous winter trek with their dog teams as they navigated through some of the densest woods in North America and over snow reaching up to six feet deep.[5]

Located at the head of the Great Lakes, the surface of Lake Superior is twenty-one feet higher than that of Lake Huron into which it flows. This difference in water levels resulted in the formation of a series of rapids in the St. Marys River abreast of Sault Ste. Marie that in time would require the construction of a shipping canal to negotiate. As a Chippewa, John Boucher was well acquainted with his people's practice of shooting these turbulent rapids by canoe—a venture known to have proved occasionally fatal. During the mid-nineteenth century, Boucher became a well-known personality to tourists when he began offering amusement rides through this stretch of whitewater. These excursions proved so popular that within a short time more than a dozen canoes piloted by local Native Americans were carrying crowds of thrill seekers through the dangerous rapids.[6] This unique trade lasted well into the early half of the twentieth century.

As noted earlier, the men operating the dog teams were often a remote settlement's only link to the outside world during wintertime. As a result, the local post office became a public meeting place to learn of the latest news. The assassination of Abraham Lincoln on April 14, 1865 represents what is perhaps the most significant episode in domestic politics during the nineteenth century. For many of those living on the frontier, the first word of this historic event arrived with the dog sled team carrying the mail. When Antoine Paquette died in July of 1906, Sault Ste. Marie's *The Evening News* reflected upon his contribution in bringing the news of Lincoln's death by stating:

> It was Antoine Paquette and the late John Boucher who brought to the Soo the news of the assassination of Abraham Lincoln in 1865. Those who were residents of the St. Marys valley will remember the excitement occasioned by the news, and not a few will feel the pang of regret that the aged pioneer has passed away.

The arrival of the first railroad into Sault Ste. Marie in 1887 did not eliminate the need for dog teams as they continued to be

While the above photograph was not taken in Michigan, dog teams such as the one depicted provided many northern communities in the state with their only link to the outside world during the long winter months. (Library of Congress)

employed carrying mail between other points in the eastern Upper Peninsula such as Whitefish Point, St. Ignace, De Tour, and Mackinac Island. Furthermore, the use of this transportation method was in no way limited to the winter months, as many owners simply replaced the runners of their sleds with wheels after the last of the snows had melted.[7]

During the coldest months of the year, the delivery of mail to Mackinac Island relied upon dog sled, horse sleigh, or a unique contraption involving a rowboat outfitted with skis. When ice first began forming between St. Ignace and the island at the beginning of winter, the mail carriers began using sleds pulled by a single dog. As the ice increased in thickness, the men added more dogs until the channel had frozen solid enough to support the weight of horse drawn sleighs. When the arrival of spring brought about thinning ice, the mail carriers assigned to this route began using the modified boat. Working in pairs, one of the men pulled from the front of the mail-laden boat while the other pushed from behind all the way across the 4 1/2 mile channel and back. Although the boat offered an added level of safety if the ice suddenly gave way, the men involved had to be ready to leap into to the craft at the first sign of danger—the coldness of the water offered very little in the way of second chances. Upon reaching solid ice, the mail carriers would exit the boat to resume pushing and pulling it to their destination. Such practices lasted well into the late 1920s.[8]

One enterprising veterinarian from Sault Ste. Marie named John F. Deadman used a dog team to make his rounds in winter. A colorful individual that once served as city treasurer, Dr. Deadman had lost one of his legs in a 1893 hunting accident—a handicap that in no way impeded his adventurous spirit. Traveling through heavy snow on nearly a daily basis, the veterinarian provided his services to locations up to one-hundred miles from his office. On one such trip to St. Ignace during the winter of 1908, John Deadman covered a distance of sixty-five miles in five and one-half hours, thus achieving an impressive average cross-country speed of nearly twelve miles per hour.[9]

On February 29, 1928, a heavy snowstorm isolated the village of De Tour and its 600 residents from the outside world. Within a few days, all of the meat and flour supplies were exhausted.[10] The very real threat of famine sparked a relief operation to send critical supplies to the snowbound community located sixty miles south of Sault Ste. Marie where the St. Marys River empties into Lake Huron. While this effort included tractors equipped with snowplows and an U.S. Army transport plane, the first load of food and medicine reached De Tour when John Deadman arrived with his dog sled team on the morning of March 16—sixteen days after the onset of the crisis. Accompanied by Fred W. Luening, a Milwaukee newspaper correspondent, Deadman's dog team had overtaken a large motorized snowplow at

71

Goetzville the previous evening while it was still about fifteen miles from their mutual destination. Relating the adverse conditions the men encountered during their perilous three-day adventure, Luening provided this brief description of his personal efforts: "Time after time I had to get off the sled and onto my snowshoes to dig out the dogs. For a time, until I became exhausted, I helped the dogs pull the sled."[11]

As nearly the entire population of the small village looked on, the army plane dispatched from Sault Ste. Marie landed on the frozen St. Marys River within a few hours of Dr. Deadman's arrival. Delivering additional food and medicine, the plane made several additional trips between the Soo and De Tour that day while also visiting some of the less stricken communities in the area.[12] His charitable task in alleviating some of the suffering endured by the residents of De Tour now complete, Fred Deadman returned to Sault Ste. Marie aboard the military cargo plane later that same day.[13]

In time, snowmobiles and other snow traversing machines supplanted the dog sled teams in supplying the dwindling number of isolated communities spread throughout the Upper Peninsula. The construction of new roads reaching into nearly every corner of the state hastened this process by pushing back the boundaries of the frontier. Today, the dog sled tradition remains alive and well in Michigan although now primarily relegated to sporting and recreational activities.

Chapter Eleven
Grand Rapids Tornado - 1912

Although the area in western Michigan that was to one day grow into the city of Grand Rapids had been inhabited for over 2,000 years by various native peoples, it was not until a Baptist missionary named Isaac McCoy arrived in 1825 that the first non-native settlement was established along the banks of the Grand River. The completion of a federal land survey in 1831 resulted in a sizable influx of people into this part of the state. Fueled in large part by settlers from New England, this expansion in population resulted in the Michigan Legislature granting the growing community a village charter in 1838. During the following twelve years, the population, commerce, and material wealth of Grand Rapids experienced a period of prosperity that resulted in its incorporation as a city on April 2, 1850.[1]

Located only twenty-five miles up the Grand River from Lake Michigan, the city was easily accessible by water transportation. In addition to the establishment of flour and lumber mills, the mid to late 1800s also saw the development of several salt and gypsum mining operations in the Grand Rapids area. Although becoming home to a number of iron works and machine shops during this same time period, the city's many furniture and cabinet manufacturers represented its most important industry. Within twenty years of the first such firms entering operation during the late 1830s, Grand Rapids, benefiting from its rail access to the important consumer markets in Chicago and the large cities of the East Coast, had grown to become one of the nation's largest furniture manufacturing centers.

So phenomenal was this expansion that by 1900 there were over fifty furniture manufacturers located in Grand Rapids, which by this time had reached a population of 87,500 citizens. Combined with other firms in the area supplying wood, metal fittings, and other materials necessary for the production of furniture this single form of industry was responsible for providing employment to nearly half of the local workforce.

On the morning of Saturday, July 13, 1912, several area farmers were gathering to sell their produce at the city market in downtown Grand Rapids. Unknown to the vendors awaiting the opening bell at 4 o'clock that morning, a massive thunderstorm was approaching unseen from the southwest. Just moments before official trading began, and with no sign of wind to announce its impending arrival, several of those in the crowd spotted a funnel shaped cloud heading directly towards the gathered wagons at the market. With little time to spare, those in the path of the tornado scrambled to whatever place of shelter they could find within the few seconds afforded them. Just before reaching the market, the funnel cloud struck the adjoining Central League Baseball Park. Tearing into the stadium's structure, the strong winds lifted the roof of the grandstand from its supports before ripping it to pieces and scattering the debris all over the market. With deadly missiles raining down from the dark skies, a panic broke out amongst the people and horses in the path of the destruction. The resulting pandemonium left at least forty persons injured and several horses dead in the devastated market.[2]

The injured included men and women knocked unconscious by panicked horses struggling to escape the storm. While a number of those involved suffered broken limbs, a vendor named Nellie Wiersma received the most serious injuries at the market that morning. When the storm struck, Wiersma struggled to calm her frightened horses as they threatened to bolt. Thrown to the ground by the nervous animals, two runaway fruit wagons ran over the helpless vendor just moments later. With serious doubts as to the prospects of her survival, rescuers removed the stricken woman to a local hospital.[3] With no reports to the contrary in subsequent newspaper reports, it appears that Nellie Wiersma managed to survive her life threatening injuries.

Leaving the wreckage of the baseball park and the chaotic devastation at the city market in its wake, the tornado continued its path of destruction as it ripped into what press reports described as the "best residence district" in Grand Rapids. The natural disaster visited upon the city that morning prompted officials to call out the fire department and the police reserves to begin the recovery effort.[4] Despite inflicting an estimated $10,000 (nearly $240,000 in 2014 dollars) in damage consisting primarily of ruined produce and wrecked wagons, the storm caused no fatalities at the market. In addition, no deaths were reported in the affected residential area, although the damages inflicted to these neighborhoods also amounted to several

201. City Market, Grand Rapids, Mich.

A postcard dated 1914 showing farmers selling produce from horse drawn wagons at the city market in Grand Rapids. (Author's Collection)

thousand dollars.[5]

The lack of fatalities can be attributed to the early hour at which the tornado struck as there were relatively few people in the city streets. There was, however, to be at least one local death indirectly attributed to the calamity visited upon Grand Rapids that summer morning. Left in a weakened state of health by a nervous condition, the ferocity of the storm affected fifty-seven year old Charles Gibbs so adversely that he died a short time later.[6]

The same storm system that slammed into Grand Rapids that July morning also caused widespread destruction in Minnesota and Wisconsin. At Minneapolis, the tempest left three dead and thirteen others injured while also inflicting over $100,000 in property damage. In Wisconsin, two people lost their lives to the storm at Eau Claire before reaching the small village of Pleasant Prairie south of Kenosha, where it caused the death of Mrs. Edward Printz along with injuring several others. Before proceeding eastward over Lake Michigan, the line of heavy weather left a trail of demolished homes, barns, downed electrical and telegraph lines, and washed out bridges throughout the affected Wisconsin countryside.[7]

While widely reported at the time as being the first tornado to strike the city of Grand Rapids, the storm of July 13, 1912 was not to be the last such event experienced by that area throughout its long history, nor would it be the most devastating. On April 3, 1956, a F5 tornado–the most violent type of this particular weather phenomenon–touched down just southwest of the city. Leveling the Grand Rapids suburbs of Hudsonville and Standale, the massive tornado left 18 dead and 340 injured. Besides Michigan, this wide-reaching storm system also spawned several tornadoes across twelve other states including Arkansas, Illinois, Indiana, Kansas, Kentucky, Mississippi, Missouri, Nebraska,

Ohio, Oklahoma, Tennessee, and Wisconsin over a two-day period.

Chapter Twelve
Deadly Windfall

On October 1, 1913, workers at the Bow, McLachlan & Company shipyard in Paisley, Scotland began final preparations to launch a steam tanker for the British shipping firm Petroleum Carriers, Limited. During the ceremonies that accompany such occasions, the steel hull of the 255-foot tanker slid uneventfully into the River Clyde. Of those present for the launching festivities that autumn day, none could have imagined that twenty-three years later this ship was to play the central character in an unusual episode in Michigan history.

With its final construction completed over the winter, the tanker entered service in 1914 as the *J. Oswald Boyd*—so named to recognize a senior member of its owning company. During World War I, the British Admiralty requisitioned the *Boyd* for use as an oiler to support the war effort. Returned to Petroleum Carriers following the end of hostilities, this ship remained active for that fleet until its sale in 1923 to the Pan American Petroleum & Transport Company of Los Angeles. This arrangement lasted for the next seven years, when, in November of 1930, the New York City based Gotham Marine Corporation purchased the *J. Oswald Boyd* for a sum of $38,600.[1]

With their new acquisition capable of passing through the locks of the old St. Lawrence River canals then in use, Gotham entered into an agreement with the Nicholson-Universal Steamship Company to operate the *J. Oswald Boyd* on the Great Lakes. Far removed from its saltwater origins, this tanker operated in the liquid bulk trade on the freshwater seas of North

America without incident for the next six years.

Loaded with 920,000 gallons of high-test aviation gasoline worth $180,000, Captain Walter M. Whitney guided the *J. Oswald Boyd* out of Indiana Harbor, Indiana on Saturday, November 7, 1936 bound for Detroit, Michigan.[2] Such a voyage requires a complete transit of Lake Michigan, the Straits of Mackinac, and Lake Huron before navigating through the St. Clair River, Lake St. Clair, and finally the upper Detroit River. By the early morning hours of the following morning, Captain Whitney—a well-seasoned veteran of the lakes with some 40 years of experience—had guided his ship into the northern reaches of Lake Michigan.

One of the most treacherous areas on the inland seas, the numerous hidden reefs and islands spread across this stretch of the lake have led to the loss of countless ships and their crews over the years. As Captain Whitney attempted to navigate the *J. Oswald Boyd* through this gauntlet, the notoriously bad weather of November on the Great Lakes complicated his efforts with a blinding snowstorm. Robbed of visibility in a time before modern navigational aids such as radar made their appearance on the lakes, Whitney soon lost his bearings as the tanker began drifting off its intended course. Hopelessly lost, the crew was unable to work their way out of this situation before feeling their ship shudder violently to a stop at 6:40 that morning as it fetched up on Simmons Reef twenty-two miles north of Beaver Island.

Sitting on an even keel and not taking on a significant amount of water, the nineteen men aboard the *Boyd* were in no immediate peril despite their ship being hard aground in unsheltered waters. About twenty minutes after the stranding, Captain Whitney used a megaphone to shout a distress call to a passing vessel, which radioed this information to the coast guard stations at Beaver Island, Grand Haven, and Mackinaw City.[3] In response, the coast guard dispatched a lifeboat from Beaver

Island and the cutter *Escanaba* from its station at Grand Haven.[4]

Arriving on the scene within six hours of the accident, the Beaver Island lifeboat returned to base a short time later carrying Oswald Emig, the stranded tanker's first mate. After contacting the operators of the *J. Oswald Boyd* to make preliminary arrangements to refloat their ship, Emig rejoined the coast guard crew on its return to the site of the stranding. Immediately after becoming aware of the problem, the management of the Nicholson-Universal Steamship Company contacted the Great Lakes Towing Company, which responded by dispatching its salvage tug *Favorite*. A veteran of countless successful salvage endeavors, the large steam tug departed its dock at Sault Ste. Marie, Michigan at 10 o'clock that evening and proceeded down the St. Marys River towards the crippled ship in northern Lake Michigan.[5]

Throughout the first day of the grounding, the crew of the *J. Oswald Boyd* worked tirelessly to keep their ship's three onboard pumps operating as heavy winds pummeled the area. Sitting atop the reef, the extreme forces exerted on the exposed ship threatened to rip it to pieces at any moment. Meanwhile, a coast guard lifeboat dispatched from Mackinac Island had joined its counterpart from Beaver Island to maintain a silent vigil alongside the black hull of the vulnerable tanker in the event it became necessary to evacuate the crew.[6] Encountering heavy seas as it steamed north from Grand Haven, the same storm conditions assaulting the *Boyd* also delayed the arrival of the cutter *Escanaba*.

Although the waters of northern Lake Michigan remained choppy on the morning of November 9, 1936, conditions had improved enough for Captain Whitney to give his 18-man crew the order to abandon ship. Climbing over the side to their wrecked ship, the men descended by ladders into the waiting coast guard lifeboats, which ferried them to Mackinaw City.

Despite the threat of their ship breaking up and possibly exploding at any second, the crew of the *J. Oswald Boyd* managed to survive the twenty-four hour duel with the elements without injury.[7]

The very real possibility of igniting the *Boyd*'s volatile cargo required the coast guard and salvage crews to observe special precautions while working around the grounded ship. Among these safety measures was a strict adherence amongst the salvagers to leave their tobacco on the *Favorite* and to use special explosion-proof flashlights to eliminate the possibility of producing any sparks. To prevent the exhaust of their engines setting fire to any of the leaking gasoline, guardsmen remained vigilant in turning off the motors of their boats while operating alongside the tanker.[8]

Having already paid at least one visit to the wreck of the *J. Oswald Boyd*, the *Favorite* returned to Simmons Reef on November 10 to continue salvage efforts. By this time, both Captain Whitney and William Pilkey, the port engineer for the Nicholson-Universal Steamship Company, had joined the crew of the wrecking tug to assist in the recovery effort.[9] It was at this time that the salvors initiated a plan to offload some of the *Boyd*'s cargo into the tanker *General Markham* in the prospect of floating the stranded ship off the reef by reducing its draft. Owned by the Cleveland Tankers fleet, the 258-foot *Markham* was en route to Indiana Harbor when it arrived on the scene. A combination of shallow water and heavy seas, however, prevented the crew of the *General Markham* from coming alongside the stranded tanker.[10] This effort having proven futile and believing further work held little hope for success, the owners attempted to minimize their losses by abandoning the wrecked steamer to the insurance underwriters the following day.[11]

Leaving the *J. Oswald Boyd* to its fate on the lonely reef, the *Favorite* steamed towards home—its crew disappointed with their failure to salvage the ship and unaware that this was just the opening chapter of a six year saga. Upon returning to Sault Ste. Marie, Captain William B. Mitchell related the dangers present around Simmons Reef by telling the local newspaper of only being able to maneuver the *Favorite* to within 800 to 900 feet of the stranded ship, while the larger *Markham* was unable to get any closer than one mile away. During the same interview, the captain of the salvage tug provided an insight into some of the damage sustained by the *J. Oswald Boyd* in the grounding by reporting its engine room flooded and that part of the ship's sizable gasoline cargo was leaking through two ruptured tanks on its port side.[12]

Almost immediately following the *Favorite*'s departure, fishermen from Beaver Island descended upon the wrecked tanker in search of free gasoline. Despite the inherit risks involved, these men commenced siphoning off the precious fuel using rudimentary equipment while observing little or no safety procedures. These activities eventually brought the fishermen into direct contact with individuals representing the underwriters, which resulted in physical altercations breaking out between the two opposing parties.[13]

Five days after the accident, representatives of the U.S. Bureau of Marine Inspection and Navigation began their investigation into the wreck of the *J. Oswald Boyd* by convening an official hearing at Sault Ste. Marie. While giving testimony before the board, Captain Whitney described how he lost his bearings in the heavy snowstorm just before his ship struck Simmons Reef. One of the questions put to the captain by the board members was whether the accident could have been avoided had his ship been fitted with wireless or direction finder equipment. Speaking of the wrecked ship and his frustration concerning the accident, Captain Whitney told the board, "She's up on that reef now, high enough to make a good lighthouse, and that's what they need there, too." In addition to Whitney, the commission also heard testimony from each of the other eighteen men aboard the tanker at the time of the stranding.[14]

On November 23, the dangers posed by the wrecked tanker became clear when one of the several local fishermen venturing to the reef suffered serious burns when gasoline fumes exploded aboard his small craft.[15] While this incident did little to deter amateurs from continuing their foolhardy salvage efforts, it foreshadowed an event of a much greater magnitude that was to have far more devastating consequences.

The most committed effort to remove the estimated 900,000 gallons of gasoline remaining aboard the wrecked tanker was that undertaken by Everett Cole, the owner of the Beaver Island Transit Company. Using his shallow draft mail boat *Rambler*, Cole managed to offload several thousand gallons of the prized cargo, which he sold to a variety of customers both on and off Beaver Island. With ice forming quickly and desiring to carry more gasoline on each trip, the enterprising businessman soon pressed his larger boat *Marold II* into service on the salvage operation.

Originally built as the *LaBelle* at Camden, New Jersey in 1911 this steel-hulled yacht was renamed *Marold II* in 1918. While moored to its dock at Marysville, Michigan in September of 1921, a massive fire broke out aboard the 129-foot vessel. Although heavily damaged by the blaze, its owner, automobile manufacturer C. Harold Wills, and the four crewmembers aboard the yacht at the time managed to escape the flames.[16] Rebuilt at Port Huron after sitting derelict for four years, the *Marold II* worked as an excursion vessel on Lake Michigan before assuming the Charlevoix to Beaver Island run in 1935.

Under unseasonably sunny skies, the *Marold II* steamed slowly away from its dock at Charlevoix at 8:15 in the morning of News Year's Day 1937. Commanded by its eighty-three year old captain, Ludlow L. Hill, the mail boat began the 40-mile journey across Lake Michigan to the wrecked *J. Oswald Boyd* under a column of smoke rising from its single stack. Also aboard the steel-hulled vessel for this fateful trip was Everett Cole, his brother Raymond, Bruce McDonough and Captain Hill's fifty-year-old son Leon. After successfully navigating through fields of drift ice, the *Marold II* finally arrived alongside the stranded tanker later that day to begin salvage operations.

During the late afternoon hours, a number of people living on Beaver Island and the Michigan mainland heard what sounded like thunder coming across the waters of Lake Michigan. A short time later, the mystery took an ominous turn when smoke was seen rising from the direction of Simmons Reef. Many of those witnessing these events soon reached the inescapable conclusion that the *Marold II* had met with misfortune while engaged in salvaging gasoline from the grounded *J. Oswald Boyd*.

After reports of these observations reached the U.S. Coast Guard station at Beaver Island, a lifeboat under the command of Captain William Ludwig set out in the gathering darkness to investigate the origin of the smoke emanating from the lake. Arriving on the scene, the guardsmen found the *Marold II* ripped to pieces by a devastating explosion that left only a portion of its bow and an even smaller section of its stern rising above the surface of the water. While the rescuers found no trace of the vessel's lifeboats, there was no evidence to suggest that any of the five men aboard the ill-fated mail boat had escaped the blast and resulting fire that continued to burn throughout the night.[17]

Within hours of the disaster, a rumor spread through Charlevoix that told of four individuals having boarded the *Marold II* as sightseers prior to its final departure from that city.[18] By the following morning, however, local officials had discounted this speculation when no one in the northern Michigan community reported any missing persons, a fact substantiated by the statements of eyewitnesses that saw only five men aboard the mail boat as it left the harbor.[19]

Although little hope remained of finding any of the missing crewmembers alive, the coast guard began an immediate search of the nearby waters. Among the assets employed in this operation was a U.S. Army biplane assigned to the 108th Observation Squadron, 33rd Division of the Illinois National Guard piloted by Captain Wilson Newhall. Leaving its base at Chicago on the morning following the accident, the aircraft encountered a snowstorm that forced Newhall to land at Brevort on the south shore of Michigan's Upper Peninsula about 20 miles northwest of the Straits of Mackinac. By the morning of Sunday, January 3, the weather had improved sufficiently for Captain Newhall and his radio operator, Elmer Isaacson, to resume their search of the area surrounding Simmons Reef. As it droned over the lake, the small aircraft carried several flying suits for its crew to drop to anyone spotted on the ice floes below. When it became obvious that no one had survived the sinking of the *Marold II*, the coast guard suspended the search and the army plane returned to Chicago.[20]

The explosion that destroyed the *Marold II* was powerful enough to blow the mail boat's top deck and pilothouse onto the deck of the *J. Oswald Boyd*. Although the fire sparked by this blast burned for several hours and heavily damaged the grounded tanker's forward section, the majority of its remaining gasoline cargo somehow managed to escape the intense inferno intact.

As all of those aboard the mail boat were residents of Beaver Island, word of the disaster devastated the small community. Searching the smoldering accident scene after the fire finally burned out, the coast guard found two badly burnt bodies amongst the twisted wreckage of the *J. Oswald Boyd*. Taken ashore, a local dentist identified the charred remains as belonging to Beaver Island Transit Company president Everett Cole and his brother Raymond.[21] Later that year, the receding ice accompanying the spring thaw revealed the presence of additional human remains aboard the abandoned tanker. While the body of Captain Hill drifted ashore on Beaver Island, the remains of his son, Leon, went missing until being found the following year in the waters of Green Bay.[22]

As winter tightened its grip on the Great Lakes region in the weeks following the *Marold II* disaster, the ice on upper Lake Michigan between Simmons Reef and the mainland became thick enough to support the weight of motor vehicles. During the middle of February, fishermen from Brevort established a 15 mile trail across the ice to the wreck. Working quietly, they managed to keep their secret for about a week and a half before word of the ice bridge spread throughout the area.[23] Lured by the prospect of obtaining free gasoline, a steady stream of humanity descended upon the *J. Oswald Boyd* like ants swarming a discarded piece of sugar—with one crucial exception: the ants need not concern themselves with the possibility of the sugar exploding at the slightest provocation!

From Sault Ste. Marie in the north to Cedarville in the east and Escanaba to the west, and all points in between, those looking to cash in on the free fuel bonanza ventured across the ice in all manner of vehicles ranging from cars and trucks to tractors and horse drawn sleighs. The methods employed during this amateurish salvage effort were foolhardy at best. Besides simple siphoning, some individuals employed open buckets suspended on ropes to lift the fuel from the wrecked tanker's hull while others used shallow pans to skim it off the surface of the ice. With little regard to the danger of igniting the gasoline fumes, many drove their vehicles right up to the side of the ship to load the precious liquid cargo. In perhaps the most blatant example of the careless attitude expressed by those involved, a home movie taken at the time includes a very brief glimpse of what appears to be a man casually smoking a cigarette as the salvage operation continues in full swing nearby.

The danger of an explosion was not the only hazard associated with the free gasoline harvest, as the trail across the ice could prove equally deadly. The perils of traveling across the frozen lake became evident on February 28, 1937 when a truck driven by Grant Brooks of Cedarville broke through the ice and sank in 27 feet of water. Drowning in the cold waters of Lake Michigan, Brooks became the sixth person to die in connection to the wreck of the *J. Oswald Boyd*. Three days later, a rescue party managed to recover the young man's body by pulling it to the surface through a hole cut in the ice. Despite its deadly outcome, this incident did little to slow the continuing salvage effort. In fact, even as work to retrieve the body of Grant Brooks from its watery tomb neared its conclusion, another truck nearly sank to the bottom of the lake when its rear wheels broke through the ice. In this case, however, nearby motorists were able to pull the partially sunken vehicle to safety.[24]

By the beginning of March, press reports were crediting the impromptu salvage effort with removing approximately 10,000 gallons of gasoline on a daily basis. Aware the ice bridge would

With its mangled superstructure providing mute testimony of the powerful explosion that destroyed the *Marold II* and killed five men, the hulk of the *J. Oswald Boyd* is the scene of frenzied activity as the local citizenry attempt to obtain free gasoline from its holds. (Author's Collection)

not last indefinitely, those engaged in this enterprise worked day and night to recover as much of the fuel as possible. By this time, however, the rising death toll along with the prospects of the hazardous endeavor leading to even more fatalities had attracted the ire of local law enforcement officials. Mackinac County Sheriff William W. McCauley became so incensed with this situation that he called upon U.S. Army officials at Selfridge Field north of Detroit to bomb the wreck of the *J. Oswald Boyd* with airplanes to prevent any further salvaging.[25] In the end, however, the army took no action and the abandoned tanker remained hard aground on Simmons Reef as a steady trail of visitors slowly removed its lucrative cargo.

Once reclaimed from the wreck, the gasoline found its way into every type of storage container imaginable, ranging from small metal cans to wooden barrels and steel drums. While many of these containers went ashore inside private automobiles, larger operations employed trucks, wagons, and sleds to move sizable quantities of fuel across the ice. Once on land, the salvaged gasoline could present some additional problems that brought its true worth into question. Contaminated with water and other impurities, many drivers using this fuel soon found themselves having trouble getting their vehicles to run properly. In addition, the massive influx of the salvaged gasoline into the Sault Ste. Marie forced that city's fire chief to embark upon a campaign to enforce the state laws governing the transportation and storage of the flammable liquid. Speaking of the dangers associated with stockpiling large quantities of gasoline in private homes and barns to the local newspaper, Chief Frank F. Trombley commented, "If a fire broke out it would be up to my men to fight it and I am thinking of their lives as well as hundreds of others."[26]

During the late spring of 1937, Joseph Beatty of De Tour along with fellow villagers Albert and William McLeod began working to release the *J. Oswald Boyd* from Simmons Reef. Despite the opinions of many experts that concluded such a feat as being impossible, the three men succeeded in refloating the twisted hull of the heavily damaged ship on June 5 of that year.[27] Towed to De Tour, they grounded the vessel on the bottom of the St. Marys River near their homes. Over the following years, the men explored a number of uses for the derelict hull, including one proposal to convert the front half of the ship into a salvage scow. In the end, however, the wrecked vessel remained resting on the bottom of the river near the small village as its owners sold or removed parts of its steel structure.[28]

Had the Second World War not intervened, it is likely that the distorted hulk of the *J. Oswald Boyd* may have continued slowly rusting away in the waters of the St. Marys River indefinitely, or at least until the authorities forced its removal. Following America's entry into the war in December of 1941, however, the demand for steel reached meteoric heights as the nation began focusing its industrial might on the war production effort. As part of its scrap metal drive, the U.S. War Production Board made arrangements with the owners of the *Boyd* to raise the derelict ship for its eventual scrapping by the Great Lakes Steel Corporation of Detroit.[29]

Raised from the river bottom in the late spring of 1942, the Woodmere Scrap Iron and Metal Company took delivery of the *J. Oswald Boyd* before arranging its final sale to the Great Lakes Steel Corporation through the Grant Iron and Metal Company.[30] Having survived a tow down the length of Lake Huron, the mangled remains of the tanker passed through the St. Clair River and across Lake St. Clair before entering the Detroit River on July 15, 1942.[31] Arriving at Detroit later that same day, the *Boyd* finally reached the city that had been its intended destination nearly six years earlier when fate intervened.

In addition to the *Marold II*, one of the vessels figuring prominently in the wreck of the *J. Oswald Boyd* was also destined to meet a tragic end. Transferred to saltwater service following the outbreak of the Second World War, the coast guard cutter *Escanaba* assumed patrol and convoy escort duties until it suddenly exploded in the North Atlantic just west of Greenland shortly after 5 o'clock in the morning of June 13, 1943. At the time, the *Escanaba* was operating with a convoy that had left Narsarssuak, Greenland three days earlier bound for St. John's, Newfoundland. Out of its complement of 105 men, only 2 were pulled from the unforgiving waters of the North Atlantic by the U.S. Coast Guard tug *Raritan*. Despite representing one of the coast guard's greatest wartime disasters in terms of lives lost, the cause of the sinking remains unexplained. It is widely believed, however, that the *Escanaba* fell victim to an enemy mine or torpedo. Prevented from leaving the lakes during the war through the efforts of the U.S. Coast Guard and the Lake Carriers Association, the salvage tug *Favorite*—the fourth such named tugboat to sail the Great Lakes—operated through 1954 before being idled by the Great Lakes Towing Company at Cleveland, Ohio. Towed to Sault Ste. Marie in 1972 for use as a museum ship, this historic vessel subsequently fell into disrepair when these plans never came to fruition. Sold for scrap in 1980, the *Favorite* met that fate at De Tour, not far from where the *J. Oswald Boyd* had spent six years grounded on the river bottom following its refloating off Simmons Reef.

Chapter Thirteen
Disaster on Easter Sunday – 1958

A proposal to build an airport to serve the Saginaw Valley that first came about during the 1930s resulted in the 1941 purchase of a square mile lot of land in Saginaw County about two miles east of Freeland. As such, this piece of property was centrally located to serve the cities of Bay City, Midland, and Saginaw. Although the onset of the Second World War did not prevent plans of building an airport to proceed, it did lead, however, to the U.S. Army taking control of the facility until the end of the conflict. On September 19, 1943, Army Air Forces General Hoyt S. Vandenberg addressed a crowd numbering some 100,000 strong that had gathered for the dedication ceremonies signifying the completion of the Tri-City Airport. Against a backdrop of 24 P-47 Thunderbolt fighter planes from Washington D.C. and 3 B-24 Liberator bombers flown in from Willow Run south of Detroit, General Vandenberg, in his post as the air forces' deputy chief of air staff, delivered an oration that, unsurprisingly, spoke highly of airpower's contribution to the war effort.[1]

Interestingly, the Tri-City Airport saw some use during the war as a prisoner of war camp to hold several thousand captured German soldiers. The end of hostilities saw the U.S. military begin a massive downsizing to reduce its size to a peacetime level. This process included the transfer of the airfield from the federal government to the airport commission established by its three owning communities on June 1, 1946.

Nearly twelve years later, on April 6, 1958, a Vickers Viscount turboprop commercial airliner operated by Capital Airlines departed Newark Airport at Newark, New Jersey as Flight 67 bound for Chicago with intermediate stops at Detroit, Flint, and Tri-City.[2] Registered as N7437 and manufactured by Vickers-Armstrongs Ltd., this aircraft's maiden flight took place at its builder's factory in southern England on August 24, 1956. Seven days later, Vickers delivered the new airliner to Capital Airlines, which placed it into service on its network of routes spanning the eastern half of the United States. The sale of an eventual 60 Viscounts to this airline beginning in 1954 represented a major coup by Vickers into a market dominated by large U.S. manufacturers.

Announcing its Easter Sunday departure at 7:16 p.m. with the distinctive whine of its four Rolls-Royce Dart turbine engines running at top speed, N7437 lifted off the runway at Newark to began its westward trek—albeit one hour and sixteen minutes behind schedule. In the cockpit of the Viscount on this particular occasion was a highly experienced flight crew consisting of Captain William J. Hull, and First Officer Earle M. Binkley. At 43 years in age, William Hull's career with Capital Airlines stretched back to 1941, during which time he had amassed over 1,700 flight hours with the Vickers Viscount. Having joined the airline just eighteen months earlier, 27 year old Earle Binkley had recorded nearly one-half of his 2,030 flight hours operating the turboprop aircraft.[3]

Heading into the Midwest, the Viscount landed first at Detroit before continuing to Flint's Bishop Airport, where arrived at 10:37 p.m. in the darkness of an early spring evening.[4] Spending little time on the ground, the airliner departed just twenty-five minutes later with forty-four passengers and three crewmembers aboard. Climbing to an altitude of 3,600 feet, the Viscount headed north to make the short 43 mile hop to the Tri-City Airport, a journey expected to take approximately 15 minutes.

While marginal, the prevailing weather in the vicinity of the Tri
-City Airport during the late hours of April 6, 1958 was well
within the limits considered as being safe to operate the Vickers
Viscount. These conditions consisted of overcast skies with a 900
-foot ceiling, a temperature of 34 degrees, light snow showers,
winds from the north-northeast at 21 mph with gusts reaching as
high as 31 mph. Unknown to Captain Hull and First Officer
Binkley as they prepared to land that night, a layer of ice was
building up along their aircraft's tail mounted horizontal
stabilizer. One of the most dreaded hazards to aviators, this
icing continued to increase second by second as the Viscount
passed through the area's snow showers. Distorting the critical
shape of the horizontal stabilizer, the ice reduced its effectiveness
by disturbing the airflow passing over the control surfaces.

Contacting the Saginaw Air Traffic Communication Station
(ATCS) at 11:16 p.m., the crew of Flight 67 radioed the ground to
report their passage over the Tri-City Airport. Circling the field
to enter the landing pattern, the Viscount signaled its arrival to
several ground witnesses that turned their attention to the
movement of the craft's lights against the black veil of night.
Watching the airliner make a left turn to line up with the
runway, these same people saw the landing lights illuminate as
the crew prepared to land. Moments later, the aircraft's turn
steepened as its crew attempted to avoid overshooting the
runway. Still under the watchful gaze of those on the ground,
the Viscount returned to level flight for a few seconds before
beginning a sudden descent towards the ground from an altitude
of several hundred feet.[5]

From such a low height, Captain Hull and First Officer Binkley
were powerless to arrest the Viscount's fall before it slammed
nose first into a muddy cornfield just less than a half mile short
of the runway. Smashing into the ground on its nose and the
leading edge of its right wing, the airliner tumbled onto its back

as the tremendous forces involved deposited airframe pieces, luggage, and bodies over a small area of the wet field. Immediately following the crash, the night sky lit up as an intense fire broke out. Seeking to destroy all in its path, this blaze caused several minor detonations as it reached small deposits of fuel remaining in and around the wrecked aircraft. Although the rescue effort began moments after the crash, it soon became obvious that no one aboard Flight 67 had survived. With crash happening on Easter Sunday night, it is unsurprising that the dead included a large number of holiday travelers.

Among the first to reach the scene was Warner Law, the owner of the farm into which the Capital Airlines Viscount crashed. Recounting his arrival at the accident site, Law told reporters, "By the time we got there, we realized everyone was gone. There was no chance of anyone getting out. The plane came in hard. It didn't fall. It ran into the ground." Joining the farmer during these early minutes was a number of relatives and friends of several passengers aboard the doomed airliner that had gathered at the airport to await its arrival.[6]

The muddy condition of the cornfield proved to be a serious handicap to the rescue effort undertaken by the Michigan State Police, Saginaw County Sheriff Department, and various fire department units dispatched from the surrounding communities. Laboring through deep mud and pooled water, the personnel attached to these departments struggled to reach the burning airliner. The extreme sponginess of the field proved so detrimental that at least one fire engine became stranded in the soft earth before reaching the scene. After pulling bodies from the wreckage, rescuers placed them into ambulances for transport to a temporary morgues set up in a hanger at the Tri-City Airport and the National Guard armory in Saginaw. Confronting the problem of having several bodies burned beyond recognition, the state police dispatched a special forensic team to assist in the identification process.[7]

While the majority of those aboard Flight 67 were residents of Michigan, the list of the dead included victims from ten other states. With Captain William Hull making his home in New Jersey and First Officer Earle M. Binkley and Hostess Ruth M. Denecke both hailing from New York, all of the Capital Airlines crewmembers came from the East Coast.[8] Thirty of the forty-four passengers killed came from Michigan, of which twenty were local residents from the communities of Bay City, Midland, and Saginaw. In addition to those killed from Michigan, the remaining passengers represented a cross-section of the country by coming from homes in the states of California, Illinois, New York, Ohio, Pennsylvania, Tennessee, Texas, West Virginia, and Wisconsin.

With many of the early reports appearing in the press seeming to indicate Captain William J. Hull had mistakenly landed short of the runway, several of his fellow pilots came forward within a few days of the accident to dispute any assertions that pilot error had caused the crash. Remembering their fallen colleague as a

A Vickers Viscount operated by Capital Airlines similar the one that crashed at Freeland on April 6, 1958. (Author's Collection)

95

"pilot's pilot," the following statements made by a few of those who had flown with Captain Hull appeared in a press report printed in the April 8, 1958 edition of Holland, Michigan's *The Holland Evening Sentinel*:

> "No one can tell me Joe Hull flew that ship into the ground," one veteran Capital captain snapped. "He was the best damned pilot on the line."
> "I've flown as his co-pilot many times," Capt. Sam Huntington of Capital recalled. "No more cautious, meticulous flier ever touched a throttle. He was fair and pleasant, but heaven help the co-pilot who goofed or got careless on a flight that Joe Hull commanded."

Just a few years prior to the fatal crash at Freeland, Captain Hull demonstrated his aerial expertise by safely landing a severly damaged Douglas DC-3 after a student pilot stalled the aircraft and put it into a spin. Serving as a Capital Airlines instructor pilot during this 1952 incident, William Hull managed to wrestle the falling aircraft back into controlled flight only after extreme aerodynamic forces had ripped away parts of its wingtips and disabled the ailerons—the latter of which controlled the airliner's turns. With one hand on the control yoke, Hull used his other hand to turn the aircraft to the desired direction by simultaneously increasing power to one of the DC-3's wing mounted engines while decreasing power to the other. In this manner, he managed to maneuver the stricken airliner through the sky and onto the runway of a nearby airfield, thus saving all those aboard.[9]

Notified of Flight 67's crash shortly after it occurred, the Civil Aeronautics Board (CAB) initiated an investigation into the accident.[10] Reaching the scene, investigators quickly established that N7437 impacted the ground in a nearly vertical angle—a fact strongly supported by the absence of any damage to a 65 foot high tree that was directly in the path of the stricken aircraft and only 148 feet from the point of impact.[11] Combing through the twisted remains of the $1.25 million aircraft, the team of experts searched for clues to the accident by performing tests on components recovered from the accident site. During this process, investigators found a malfunctioning nose gear Dowmic switch among the wreckage. As this device armed a stall warning system incorporating a stick shaker feature designed to alert the pilots of their aircraft beginning to lose sufficient lift to remain airborne, the possibility existed that its failure would have robbed the pilots of this critical warning during the approach into Tri-City.

In addition, the detector unit of the crashed aircraft's stall warning system had been replaced at some point before the accident. With the process used to conduct this repair failing to include the test flights necessary to calibrate the newly installed equipment, investigators could not rule out the possibility of the unit not warning the pilots of an impending stall even if the Dowmic switch functioned correctly.[12]

Although the crash took place in darkness, the CAB investigation benefited from having a large number of eyewitnesses to interview. While none of these individuals could testify as to having actually seen the aircraft itself, they did observe its lights and sounds of its engines. Amongst these witnesses was a commercial airline pilot that told investigators of the Capital Airlines Viscount entering into a bank of between 50 and 60 degrees while trying to line up on the runway. This same person also stated that after rolling out of the turn, the airliner's nose pitched down and descended steeply into the ground. At least four of the people to witness the crash saw the Viscount return to level flight for a period ranging from between four and six seconds before beginning its fatal plunge.[13]

Responding to questions put forth by the CAB on July 9, 1958, Earl Raymond, the director of maintenance for Capital Airlines, testified that his company did not recognize an inoperative stick shaker aboard its fleet of Viscounts as a "no go" item at the time of the Freeland crash. In spite of statements provided by the airliner's manufacturer that its design incorporated a number of devices to warn pilots of an impending stall, the CAB acted prudently by instructing Capital Airlines to designate a faulty stick shaker as a "no go" item effective June 27 of that year. The inoperative stall warning equipment notwithstanding, investigators heard the testimony of at least one expert witness who believed it unlikely that the airliner entered a stall before crashing.[14]

Proof of the icing conditions near the Tri-City Airport on the night of the accident came from the crew of a Lockheed Constellation operated by Capital Airlines that landed just minutes before Flight 67's scheduled arrival time. While appearing before the accident board on June 3, 1958, Flight Engineer Robert F. Higgins testified that the air heater intakes for his aircraft's four engines were among the areas found covered with ice after landing.[15] Although the prevailing weather conditions at the time of the accident along with the testimony of the Constellation's flight engineer provided a compelling case of ice having played a major role in bringing down Flight 67, the initial accident investigation failed to recognize its full significance.

As part of its attempt to determine whether icing had been a factor in the crash, the board commissioned a series of wind tunnel and flight tests to examine this possibility. While these trials revealed that a buildup of ice on the wings caused a loss of lift and an increase in drag, they also demonstrated no other significant changes to the aircraft's flight characteristics. Furthermore, a series flight tests designed to examine the stall characteristics of the Vickers Viscount in various flight profiles, including bank angles approximating those flown by the crew of

Flight 67 during the approach to the Tri-City Airport, demonstrated the test aircraft's ability to respond normally to a pilot's recovery actions.[16]

On April 15, 1959, just nine days following the one-year anniversary of the accident, the Civil Aeronautics Board released its report detailing the crash of Flight 67. Basing its opinions on the evidence and testing available at the time, the investigation board provided the following statement at the conclusion of this report:

> The probable cause of this accident was a stall during a steep turn resulting in an over-the-top entry to a spin at an altitude too low to effect recovery. Contributing factors were an inoperative stall warning device, gusty winds, and possible ice accretion on the airframe.[17]

This brief statement was not, however, to be the CAB's final word concerning the Easter Sunday crash at Freeland. On January 29, 1963, a Vickers Viscount operated by Continental Airlines crashed at Kansas City with a loss of eight lives. The resulting investigation revealed that an undetected build-up of ice on the horizontal stabilizer combined with a specific airspeed and landing configuration resulted in a sudden loss of pitch control.[18] This accident, in conjunction with at least two other similar incidents in which the pilots managed to land safely, prompted the Civil Aeronautics Board to reopen the investigation into the crash of Flight 67. Weighing the original evidence against the similarities with the other occurrences, the CAB released a revised accident report on February 17, 1965 specifying a amended probable cause identical to that of the Kansas City crash.[19] Although the disaster at Freeland made headlines in newspapers around the nation just seven years earlier, the release of the revised report went largely unnoticed by the press.

Renamed the MBS International Airport in 1994, the airport at Freeland continues to serve the cities of Bay City, Midland, and Saginaw in addition to the surrounding area stretching into the Thumb of Michigan. With a strong general aviation presence and connections to a number of major airline hubs, the airfield handles over 50,000 aircraft movements annually. The Vickers Viscount continued providing dependable service for Capital Airlines until its merger with United Airlines in June of 1961. Repainted in United colors, the surviving fleet of turboprop airliners remained in operation until being phased out in 1969.

Chapter Fourteen
Abraham Lincoln Visits Kalamazoo – 1856

The 1856 presidential election came during one of the most contentious periods in the history of the United States. A long simmering divide between the northern and southern states concerning the issue of slavery was threatening to tear the nation apart as both sides became entrenched in their opposing viewpoints. With its economy dependent upon the institution of slavery, the South bitterly opposed any outside interference by factions within the northern states seeking to curtail or abolish one of the fundamental pillars of its society. Many of the tensions concerning this debate came to a head in 1854 when Congress passed the Kansas-Nebraska Act, which not only created these two territories but also opened them to the spread of slavery by popular consent. Representing a turning point in political history of the United States, the passage of this act served to galvanize the abolitionist movement while also splitting the Democratic and Whig parties.

In early 1854, the Anti-Nebraska factions joined forces to form what was to become the Republican Party when they held their first meeting at Ripon, Wisconsin. Quickly gaining popularity, some 10,000 people attended the party's first official convention at Jackson, Michigan on July 6 of that same year. Confronted with a large crowd and sweltering summer heat, the organizers of this event moved it to an oak grove just outside of town, thereby designating the birthplace of the Republican Party as "Under the Oaks."

During its first national convention at Philadelphia,

Pennsylvania in June of 1856, the Republican Party nominated former California governor John C. Frémont as its presidential candidate in that year's election. Meanwhile, former U.S. senator William L. Dayton of New Jersey garnered 253 votes during the first ballot for the vice-president nomination. Finishing the initial contest in second place with 110 votes, Dayton's closest rival was a relatively unknown country lawyer from Springfield, Illinois named Abraham Lincoln. Benefiting from additional support, Dayton easily secured the party's vice-president nomination with an overwhelming victory in the formal vote.

Among the party of Michigan delegates attending the convention was Hezekiah Wells, a prominent lawyer and former circuit judge from Kalamazoo. Upon returning to Michigan, Wells became chairman of a committee formed to organize a Frémont campaign rally in his hometown. Making good use of the party's campaign slogan, "Free speech, free press, free soil, free men, and Frémont," the group proceeded to schedule a mass meeting of Republicans for August 27, 1856 in Kalamazoo's Bronson Park.[1]

While the committee sent invitations to several well-known political personalities across the nation, Abraham Lincoln was to be the event's only out of state speaker. Although having served four terms in the Illinois State Legislature and one term in the U.S. House of Representatives, Lincoln was virtually unknown in Michigan at the time. His presence at Kalamazoo that day owes itself to a written invitation dated July 24 from Hezekiah Wells. Deeply involved in the political maneuvering then taking place in Illinois to unite the supporters of American Party candidate Millard Fillmore behind the Frémont campaign, a hesitant Lincoln could not commit to making an appearance at the rally. Along with the Michigan speaking invitation, the future president also turned down two similar overtures to address political meetings in Iowa—one such refusal based in part on what he termed as "superstition."[2]

By August 21, 1856, however, it appears that Abraham Lincoln had changed his mind about attending out of state political events when he penned a second reply to Hezekiah Wells:

> Springfield, Ills. Augt. [sic] 21, 1856
>
> Hon: H. G. Wells
> Dear Sir:
>
> At last I am able to say, no accident preventing, I will be with you on the 27th. I suppose I can reach in time, leaving Chicago the same morning. I shall go to the Matteson House, Chicago, on the evening of the 26th.
>
> Yours Truly,
> A. LINCOLN

With the appointed day rapidly approaching, preparations for the Kalamazoo meeting entered their final phase. In addition to Abraham Lincoln, the committee also received favorable responses to its invitations from a number of Michigan speakers, among which included Governor Kinsley S. Bingham and a distinguished Republican from Detroit named Zachariah Chandler.[3] Although the absence of many prominent figures promised in the weeks leading up to the event proved somewhat disappointing, it did little to dampen the festive mood of the occasion. So unknown was Lincoln in Michigan, that one of the few newspapers to provide advance notice of his scheduled appearance mistakenly printed his name as "H. Lincoln, of Illinois."[4]

As the sun began its slow rise above the eastern horizon on the morning of August 27, 1856, a 32 cannon salute announcing the beginning of the Republic convention resounded through the streets of Kalamazoo as it shattered the peaceful quietness of daybreak. By eight o'clock that summer morning, the streets became jammed with people arriving in the city to participate in

A portrait of Abraham Lincoln taken at Pittsfield, Illinois in September of 1858 some two years after he spoke at Kalamazoo. This speech is the only known public appearance made by Lincoln in Michigan during his political career. (Library of Congress)

that day's events. Forming a long procession, and accompanied by ten bands playing music, the delegates soon began a march through the banner-laden streets towards Bronson Park. Complementing the instrumental melodies of the bands were songs performed by members of the Detroit and Battle Creek Glee clubs.[5]

Appearing in front of the crowd gathered in the park at eleven o'clock, Hezekiah Wells gave a short speech commemorating the opening of the convention before introducing Zachary Chandler, the first speaker of the day. Living up to his well-earned reputation of delivering long-winded orations, the former mayor of Detroit spoke for nearly two hours. As one writer observed, Chandler's lengthy speech concluded when the meeting broke for lunch at one o'clock in the afternoon "with three times three rousing cheers."[6]

Leaving Chicago at 8:30 that same morning aboard a train operated by the Michigan Central Railroad, Abraham Lincoln did not arrive in Kalamazoo until 1:30 in the afternoon.

Meanwhile, the crowd that had dispersed for lunch began the slow process of reassembling to await the resumption of the political rally. Having rushed from the train station, Lincoln arrived at Bronson Park in time to be the first guest speaker introduced following the opening of the afternoon session. It was at 2 o'clock on that hot summer day that Abraham Lincoln gave what is widely believed to have been his only public speech ever made in the state of Michigan.[7]

Standing atop one of the four stages specifically built in the park for the occasion, the speech prepared by Abraham Lincoln concentrated primarily upon the slavery issue, with a special emphasis placed towards the intense debate concerning the possible spread of that institution into the new territories. Highlighting the single most divisive issue of the day, the future president commented, "The question of slavery, at the present day, should be not only the greatest question, but very nearly the sole question." While maintaining a political position in direct opposition to prevailing attitudes in the southern states, Lincoln expressed a somewhat conciliatory tone when he remarked, "And here let me say, that in intellectual and physical structure, our Southern brethren do not differ from us. They are, like us, subject to passions, and it is only their odious institution of slavery, that makes the breech between us."

To reinforce his stance on the key issue of slavery, Abraham Lincoln made a comparison of the northern states with both Canada and the South by arguing, "We find a people on the Northeast, who have a different government from ours, being ruled by a Queen. Turning to the South, we see a people who, while they boast of being free, keep their fellow beings in bondage. Compare our Free States with either, shall we say here that we have no interest in keeping that principal alive? Shall we say, "Let it be?" No—we have an interest in the maintenance of the principles of the Government, and without this interest, it is worth nothing."

In spite of his anti-slavery beliefs, Abraham Lincoln nonetheless held the opinion that the Constitution protected it in places where it already existed. As a result, his primary consideration was to stop its spread into the new territories. Furthermore, Lincoln disliked the destabilizing nature of abolitionist agitation and would in years to come make a deliberate effort to remove such influences from the Republican Party. Trying to distance presidential candidate John C. Frémont from any connection to the abolitionist movement during his Kalamazoo speech, Lincoln stated emphatically, "Our adversaries charge Frémont with being an abolitionist. When pressed to show proof, they frankly confess that they can show no such thing. They run off upon the assertion that his supporters are abolitionists."

Even though the dark days of the Civil War still hung five years in the future, signs of the country tearing itself apart were readily apparent in 1856. Calling attention to the very real possibility of the Union dissolving from within, the only out of state speaker at Kalamazoo that day presented the uncertain future of the nation to the audience with the following challenge, "How is the dissolution of the Union to be consummated? They tell us that the Union is in danger. Who will divide it? Is it those who make the charge? Are they themselves the persons who wish to see this result? A majority will never dissolve the Union. Can a minority do it?" As the speech reached its conclusion, Abraham Lincoln demonstrated his proficient oratory skills that would serve him so well in the future by pleading, "Don't interfere with anything in the Constitution. That must be maintained, for it is the only safeguard of our liberties. And not to Democrats alone do I make this appeal, but to all who love these great and true principles."

In spite of the disappointment generated by the absence of

several prominent speakers, Abraham Lincoln appears to have been very well received, a fact duly reflected by one *Kalamazoo Gazette* reporter devoting nearly half of his column to "the only foreign speaker in attendance." Despite the strong possibility that Lincoln made two additional addresses that day—one in Court House Square and another at Fireman's Hall—there is no recorded evidence of what he said at either of these places if such speeches did in fact take place.[8]

Echoing the politically charged atmosphere surrounding this event, the number of people said to have attended the Kalamazoo rally on August 27, 1856 varies widely depending upon the source. With the state's Republican newspapers proclaiming the event as a "Great Mass Convention of the Republican Young Men of Michigan," some of these publications estimated the crowd to have numbered at least 30,000 people. Where the Republican press had a clear incentive to capitalize upon the size of the Kalamazoo convention, Democratic newspapers had an equally compelling motive to downplay the event's popularity. As such, these publications printed widely varying attendance figures ranging from 5,000 to 15,000, along with a plethora of politically motivated commentary, including one correspondent's wry observation, "They made a great deal of noise and confusion, but accomplished nothing else."[9]

Where Abraham Lincoln spent the night after delivering his Kalamazoo speech is uncertain, but he most likely slept across the street from Bronson Park in the home of Hezekiah Wells. Possibly using the morning hours of the following day to call upon local politicians, Lincoln left the city aboard the afternoon train bound for Chicago.[10]

Of the more than fifty speeches made by Abraham Lincoln throughout the 1856 campaign season, only his address to the Republican rally at Kalamazoo found its way into print. Appearing in the August 29, 1856 edition of the *Detroit Daily*

Advertiser, the text of Lincoln's speech became lost to history until its discovery by Lincoln researcher Thomas I. Starr amongst the newspaper's historical records during the spring of 1930. Learning soon afterwards of a colleague's intention to use the speech in a forthcoming book, Starr did not publish his find until 1941.

Of the thousands gathered to hear Abraham Lincoln speak at Kalamazoo on the afternoon of August 27, 1856, none could have imagined that they were looking upon the man that within four short years was to become one of the nation's greatest presidents and one that faced challenges unlike any before or since. Elected president in November of 1860, Abraham Lincoln left Springfield, Illinois in February of the following year bound for Washington. While his journey to assume the presidency included stops in several major cities along the way, the route taken by Lincoln bypassed the state of Michigan.

Proving unpopular for most of his two consecutive terms in office, Abraham Lincoln guided the nation through the trying years of the Civil War only to fall victim to an assassin's bullet as that conflict entered its final days. Following his death, the government arranged to have a special train convey Lincoln's body back to Springfield for burial. Traversing seven northern states and viewed by countless thousands on its 1,600-mile journey, the train generally retraced the path taken by the fallen leader during his 1861 trip to the nation's capital. Consequently, the funeral train never entered Michigan during its twelve-day trek to Illinois with a brief stop at Michigan City, Indiana representing its closest approach to the state line. Having previously been a forgotten footnote in the Abraham Lincoln's political career, his untimely death imparted a renewed significance to the day he spoke at the Republican political rally at Kalamazoo.

Chapter Fifteen
The St. Clair Tunnel – 1891

Experiencing a period of rapid expansion following its 1852 founding, the Grand Trunk Railway of Canada had grown by 1880 to connect Chicago with the East Coast of the United States. Extending from the largest city in the Midwest, this rail line traversed northern Indiana and Michigan's Lower Peninsula before crossing into Canada, where it ran along the southern reaches of Ontario prior to reentering the United States. While providing dependable rail service to commerce in the region, the economic potential of this route was limited by the necessity of having to cross the St. Clair River between the cities of Port Huron, Michigan and Sarnia, Ontario.

To negotiate this natural barrier, the railroad relied upon a fleet of car ferries to move its trains across the narrow but rapidly moving river. Beginning in 1872, Grand Trunk operated a series of such vessels—among which included a swing ferry propelled solely by the river current—between its docks at Fort Gratiot on the American shore and Point Edward on the Canadian side of the river near the location at which the twin spans of the Blue Water Bridge stand today.[1] Consequently, the capacity and turnaround rates of the ferries dictated the amount of daily rail traffic moving across the international border. With traffic growing steadily throughout the mid to late 1800s, the ferry operation quickly proved inadequate to meet the increasing demand placed on the route. Traffic statistics for railcar movements across the St. Clair River during 1888 reflect the scope of the difficulties faced by Grand Trunk managers. In that year, company ferries carried 297,000 freight cars, 28,000 passenger cars, and 8,000 baggage and mail cars between the Fort Gratiot and Point Edward docks. As ice often clogged the narrow river channel throughout winter and the early months of spring, the significance of this traffic volume assumes an even greater magnitude.

In exploring solutions to this bottleneck, Grand Trunk officials found themselves confronted by a number of obstacles, which left them with few options. Heavy ship traffic on the St. Clair River—reputed as being one the most heavily traveled waterways in the world at the time—precluded the possibility of building any type of draw or swing bridge across the bustling shipping channel. Furthermore, the area's flat terrain also complicated any proposals for a suspension bridge by requiring extremely long approaches to reach a height sufficient to clear the river traffic—a feature certain to increase the overall cost of the project.[2]

With the construction of a bridge or expansion of the ferry service deemed impractical, Sir Henry Whatley Tyler, president of the Grand Trunk Railway, first floated the idea of building a rail tunnel under the St. Clair River during the late months of 1879. In October 1884, the railroad went forward with a plan to construct a tunnel by establishing the St. Clair Frontier Tunnel Company in Canada, a move followed exactly two years later by the founding of the Port Huron Railroad Tunnel Company in Michigan. Just one month later, in November of 1886, a merger of these two companies resulted in the formation of the St. Clair Tunnel Company.[3] The responsibility to head this project fell upon the railroad's chief engineer, Joseph Hobson, who had previously served in that same capacity with the Great Western Railway prior to its merger with Grand Trunk in 1882.

Tunneling through the soft sediments below the St. Clair River, however, presented several major problems, some of which required solutions never attempted before in the construction of a subaqueous railroad tunnel. To establish the characteristics of the materials lying below the river bottom, Joseph Hobson and his assistant, Thomas E. Hillman, made a series of borings in the river from a scow at spots just fifty feet south of the tunnel's intended path. Examining these samples, the engineers discovered that directly below the sandy river bottom was a mixture of quicksand and blue clay approximately ten feet deep, beneath which a twenty-one foot layer of blue clay rested upon a strata of shale.[4]

The survey results prompted Hobson to approach Henry Tyler with a proposal to bore an experimental drift along the tunnel's intended path to test different methods of working through the clay.[5] Planning to build a tunnel with an outside diameter of 25 feet and lined with bricks, the St. Clair Tunnel Company contracted the firm of William Sooysmith & Company to sink of single shaft on each side of the river in November of 1886 at a cost of $59,200. Beginning in December of that year, this project included the boring of an 8-foot diameter drift running along the center of the route chosen for the railroad tunnel. When the drift extending from the shaft dug at Port Huron encountered soft clay after covering a distance of only 33 feet, however, Sooysmith shifted all work to the Canadian side.

Having begun their effort on March 7, 1887, workers tunneling from the Sarnia shaft had extended a drift measuring some 278 feet towards the opposite shore when they encountered a natural gas pocket on April 15. With further excavation halted, the experimental tunnel soon filled with water. On May 9, work resumed when a Sooysmith crew began pumping out the flooded tunnel works. Just two days later, however, a lantern's open flame caused an explosion that resulted in some minor injuries among the workmen. Although men toiled in the tunnel throughout the following two months, all further work was

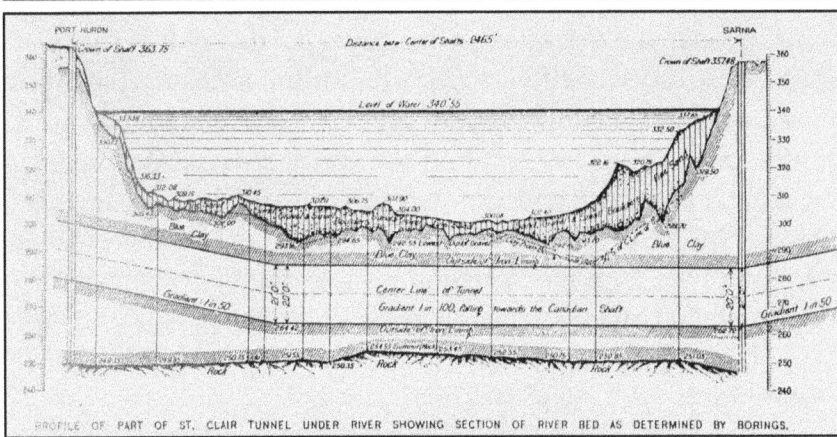

PROFILE OF PART OF ST. CLAIR TUNNEL UNDER RIVER SHOWING SECTION OF RIVER BED AS DETERMINED BY BORINGS.

A diagram illustrating the narrow band of clay between the muddy river bottom and the underlying layer of rock through which workers bore the St. Clair Tunnel. (Library of Congress)

permanently suspended on July 19, 1887. As a result, William Sooysmith & Company ended the project with a loss of $5,482 and the forfeiture of a $15,000 performance bond.[6]

When the St. Clair Tunnel Company chose to proceed with the project on its own accord, Chief Engineer Hobson ordered another series of borings to create a more accurate picture of the river bottom and underlying layers of sediment. Performed between May and July of 1888, a total of 110 borings were obtained from the river bottom—during which time passing ships struck the scow obtaining the samples on several occasions. The results of this survey allowed Hobson to determine the best possible course for the railroad tunnel through the clay below the fast moving waters of the St. Clair River. Reviewing the factors involved, Joseph Hobson placed an initial cost estimate for the project at $2,370,000.

The composition of the sediments lying below the river convinced Engineer Hobson of the necessity to employ the tunneling shield process in excavating the railroad tunnel.[7] Such a plan called for a pair of tunneling shields to bore their way from each shore to a meeting point below the middle of the St.

113

Clair River. In addition to the shields, the railroad's chief engineer also decided to use cast iron for the tunnel walls rather than a masonry lining. Besides making waterproofing a much simpler task, the use of cast iron over brick reduced the tunnel's overall bore diameter to twenty-one feet—a four foot savings. During the latter part of February 1888, Grand Trunk entered into a contract with the Hamilton Bridge and Tool Company for two tunneling shields. Taking the cost of the shields and cast iron lining into consideration, Joseph Hobson revised his initial cost estimate to $2,650,000 on July 3, 1889.

Abandoning an effort to begin tunneling from a new pair of shafts sunk near each side of the riverbank during the spring of 1888, Hobson shifted his focus to bore the tunnel from open cuts made further back from the shoreline. Commencing in January of the following year, the excavation of the cut on the Port Huron side began approximately 1,800 feet away from the river while that on the Canadian side was situated some 2,000 feet inland. With the approach cuts completed, tunneling from the Michigan side began on July 11, 1889. On September 24, nearly eleven weeks after tunneling began at Port Huron, identical work commenced on the opposite side of the river following a delay caused by a landslide at the Sarnia cut. Throughout construction, the St. Clair Tunnel Company employed an average of 700 men on the tunnel project.[8]

Using the tunneling shield method allowed workers to remove soil and install the prefabricated cast iron wall sections as the cylindrical shaped device inched its way forward through the earth below the river bottom. The tunnel lining consisted of rings assembled from 13 curved sections and a key piece. Measuring 4 feet 15/16 inches in length and 18 ¼ inches wide, each of the 2-inch thick ring sections weighed between 1,000 and 1,050 pounds. To prevent corrosion, crews working outside the tunnel entrance heated the cast iron sections before dipping them into cold tar–a process found to produce superior results over submerging cold segments into hot tar. Once inside the tunnel, workers formed a ring by moving each section into place with the aid of a circular crane that revolved around the center of the shield. Held together with 56 bolts, each ring required an additional 157 bolts to attach it to the preceding ring. Altogether, Grand Trunk's foundry at Hamilton, Ontario supplied one-third of the 50,076 ring segments and 3,852 keys fabricated for the project, with the balance coming from the Detroit Wheel & Foundry Company of Detroit. As the borehole measured 6 inches larger in circumference than the rings, workmen forced cement into this gap to prevent the tunnel from shifting. Taken as a whole, the tunnel lining weighed a respectable 28,000 tons.[9]

Reaching the river, engineers employed compressed air to relieve pressure on the tunneling shields as they bore through the surrounding clay. The application of this tunneling

A contemporary illustration of the tunneling shield inching its way below the St. Clair River. (Library of Congress)

technique—the use of which Chief Engineer Hobson had initially opposed—required the construction of airtight bulkheads at both tunnel openings, each of which had an air chamber 7 feet in diameter and 17 feet in length through which a single railroad track passed. Past the bulkhead, all work in the tunnel progressed in a compressed air environment that saw its pressure gradually increased as tunneling continued to reach 37 pounds per square inch, or 2 ½ times normal air pressure, by the time both shields met. The use of compressed air in the project began on April 7 and May 20, 1890 on the American and Canadian sides respectively.[10]

The correct alignment of the tunneling shields as they worked towards a predestined meeting point 50 feet below the surface of the St. Clair River represented one of the most critical and challenging aspects of the tunnel's construction. As any significant deviation along the 6,000-foot long excavation carried the very real consequence of the project's failure, the accuracy of the shield's movements became a major concern in the mind of Chief Engineer Hobson. To ensure the accurate positioning of the tunneling shields, workers installed an instrument station containing custom-built theodolites with telescopic sights at each of the tunnel's entrances. To ensure an unobstructed line of sight to the opposite side of the river, the St. Clair Tunnel Company purchased and demolished a house interfering with its view from the Port Huron tunnel entrance. Responsibility for the tunnel's vertical and horizontal alignment fell upon First Assistant Engineer Thomas E. Hillman and Second Assistant Engineer M. S. Blaiklock. Requiring highly precise measurements and calculations, the efforts of these two men proved amazingly accurate as when the tunneling crews met on August 30, 1890 they found only a ¼-inch vertical misalignment between the two shields.[11]

The completion of the boring operation in no way signaled the end of the project as it was to be nearly fourteen months before the first freight train passed through the new tunnel. Continuing their work, crews did not complete the tunnel's lining until one month after the two shields had met. Following the last use of compressed air on October 2, 1890, workmen began dismantling the airtight bulkheads and laying a brick foundation for the single set of track running the length of the tunnel. As Grand Trunk had previously experienced problems with its bridges from salt brine leaking from refrigerated boxcars, Chief Engineer Hobson had an extra layer of cement applied to all of the tunnel's brickwork in an effort to protect its cast iron lining from corrosion. In addition, the upper sections of the tunnel received a coating of asphalt paint to provide a layer of protection against the exhaust of coal-fired steam locomotives.[12]

With the construction project entering its final stage, Grand Trunk scheduled the St. Clair Tunnel's official dedication ceremony for Saturday, September 19, 1891—a date selected to accommodate company president Sir Henry Tyler's return to England later that month. The unfinished state of the tunnel and the persistent threat of landslides at each of its entrances, however, precluded any major public involvement in these festivities. The night before the dedication, executives of the Grand Trunk Railroad and the St. Clair Tunnel Company along with a group composed of prominent civic leaders and officials from both local and state governments attended a large banquet held at Port Huron. Among those in attendance at this event was Michigan Governor Edward B. Winans. The following morning, the formal dedication of the St. Clair Tunnel took place when a train carrying a party composed of several company officials and invited guests made the inaugural passage through the new tunnel from Sarnia to Port Huron.[13]

Anxious to abandon the costly and time-consuming ferry operation, Grand Trunk sent its first freight train through the St.

Clair Tunnel on October 24, 1891 and inaugurated passenger service on December 7 of that same year. Cutting two hours off the travel time between Chicago and Toronto, the new tunnel allowed Grand Trunk to save $50,000 a year on the operational costs of the ferries. On January 20, 1892, some two and one-half years after tunneling first began at Port Huron, the St. Clair Tunnel company declared all work on the project completed at a cost of $2,700,000—Chief Engineer Joseph Hobson's July 1889 estimate of $2,650,000 had proven prophetic.[14]

To move railcars efficiently through the tunnel, the St. Clair Tunnel Company acquired four steam locomotives from the Baldwin Locomotive Works of Philadelphia, Pennsylvania. These custom-built units were capable of operation in either direction, thereby eliminating the need of turning them around after each tunnel passage. Designed to burn anthracite coal in an effort to minimize smoke in the confines of the tunnel, each of the locomotives had sufficient power to pull a 760-ton train up the 2 percent grade at both ends of the St. Clair Tunnel. While proving effective in their assigned role, these units had a reputation of being rather slow in making progress up the inclines with a full load.[15]

Despite efforts to minimize the amount of smoke generated by the locomotives, exhaust fumes in the St. Clair Tunnel represented a deadly danger to both the employees of Grand Trunk and its passengers. The primary hazard came from the presence of carbon dioxide and carbon monoxide, both of which were deadly gasses produced by the steam engines regardless of the fuel they used. This danger compelled the installation of a ventilation system that normally took forty-five minutes to expel the harmful gasses left by a train passage. While most of the trains using the tunnel to bypass the St. Clair River made the trip without incident, it nonetheless became a common occurrence for cars to become uncoupled while ascending the grade leading

This early 1900s view shows one of the original steam locomotives in the Port Huron entrance to the St. Clair Tunnel. (Library of Congress)

to the surface. In such instances, the conductor and brakeman in their assigned stations in the caboose at the rear of the train could find themselves trapped in the gas-filled tunnel before the ventilation system had time to be effective. The danger of being overcome by the deadly fumes also applied to the engineer and fireman aboard the locomotive when they reentered the tunnel to retrieve the lost cars.[16]

The dangers of gas in the St. Clair Tunnel led to at least three accidents between 1892 and 1904 that together cost the lives of ten men. The first of these incidents took place just eleven days after the tunnel's completion when a conductor died after he and brakeman were overcome by noxious fumes on January 31, 1892. A little less than six years later, on November 28, 1897, a concentration of deadly exhaust gasses in the tunnel left three men dead. The third, and most serious of these accidents, occurred on October 9, 1904 when six men lost their lives in the

St. Clair Tunnel. The dead included two brakemen, two conductors, an engineer, and Alexander S. Begg, the superintendent of Grand Trunk's Port Huron and Sarnia terminals.[17]

The third disaster prompted Grand Trunk's decision to eliminate the dangers posed by the steam locomotives by converting to electrically powered units—a move that was to improve both the tunnel's safety and increase its capacity. This conversion included the installation of electrical equipment for the locomotives along with that to operate pumps for drainage and light the passenger stations, roundhouse, and tunnel. Altogether, the electrification project involved a 4-mile zone and 12 miles of track. As part of this major investment, the St. Clair Tunnel Company built a brick powerhouse in Port Huron on the banks of the St. Clair River about 100 feet from the centerline of the tunnel. Coal destined for the plant's four boilers arrived on a spur line from a nearby Grand Trunk track. The facility's relative location to the water's edge, however, also made it possible to receive coal from lake ships. The powerhouse remained operational until the Detroit Edison Company began supplying electricity in May 1917, after which the St. Clair Tunnel Company dismantled its generating equipment.[18]

To replace its steam locomotives, the St. Clair Tunnel Company acquired three electrically powered units built by a partnership between the electrification project's primary contractor, the Westinghouse Electric & Manufacturing Company, and the Baldwin Locomotive Works. Each of the locomotives consisted of two identical half-units featuring three 250 hp motors linked to an equal number of axles, thereby providing a complete unit with a 1,500 hp rating. In this configuration, the locomotives were capable of reaching speeds of 30 mph on level ground and 10 mph while pulling a 1,000-ton train up a 2 percent grade. The first passage of a train employing one of the new electric locomotives took place on February 20, 1908. After running side by side with the steam locomotives for nearly three months, the new system of electrically powered units went into continuous service on May 17 of that same year. During the early years of this operation, two half-units normally handled freight traffic, while passenger trains—with their lighter loads—usually only required a single half-unit to make a tunnel transit. To accommodate heavier trains and increase capacity even further, the St. Clair Tunnel Company expanded its fleet of electric locomotives with the purchase of three additional units in 1927.[19]

During the First World War, a group of conspirators led by a German national living in Detroit named Albert Kaltschmidt targeted the St. Clair Tunnel as part of a plot involving the sabotage of several local structures in both the United States and Canada. Having been under surveillance for some time, federal agents arrested Kaltschmidt shortly after the United States

One of the electric locomotive units purchased by the St. Clair Tunnel Company following its decision to electrify the tunnel after gasses from steam locomotives caused a series of fatal accidents. (Library of Congress)

entered the war in 1917. In December of that same year, the German businessman, along with five other defendants went on trial in Detroit. Found guilty on December 22, 1917, a federal judge sentenced Albert Kaltschmidt to the maximum sentence allowed under the statute of four years imprisonment and a $20,000 fine. With the exception of one individual who had turned state's evidence, the jury also returned guilty verdicts against all of Kaltschmidt's co-defendants, which, like their leader, also received the harshest sentences permitted by law. In the end, the St. Clair Tunnel remained operational throughout the war with Albert Kaltschmidt spending a little more than 3 years in federal prison before the Justice Department ordered his release and deportation to Germany in February of 1921.[20]

The outbreak of the Second World War brought about new fears of foreign agents targeting the St. Clair Tunnel. Although a highly visible target with direct implications to the success of the war effort, only one incident of suspected sabotage against the important rail tunnel is known to have taken place throughout the long conflict. On the night of June 15, 1940, a guard working for Canadian National discovered a fire in a railway freight car carrying four aircraft engines from the Glendale Motors Company at Kenna, Montana, to the Fleet Aircraft Corporation at Fort Erie, Ontario. Quickly extinguishing the flames before they caused any significant damage, the guard discovered that someone had shoved strips of a blanket soaked in a flammable liquid through holes in the floor of the car before setting them afire. The knowledge that a shipment of ammunition and explosives had passed through the tunnel just 30 minutes earlier, however, left railroad officials wondering whether the perpetrators of this act had mistakenly targeted the wrong train. The resulting investigation into this incident by law enforcement agencies from both sides of the border failed to identify any of the culprits involved.[21]

When Canadian National Railways acquired all of the Grand Trunk Railway of Canada's assets following its 1923 bankruptcy, the St. Clair Tunnel Company continued operating as an independent subsidiary of its new owning company. Lasting thirty-five years, this arrangement ended on March 31, 1958 when a corporate reorganization resulted in the company becoming a division of Canadian National. That same year also saw the retirement of the long-serving electric locomotives after a prolonged period of rising operational costs. Following the final passage of a train pulled by such a unit on September 28, 1958, all traffic through the St. Clair Tunnel switched to using standard diesel-electric locomotives—a move requiring the installation of a new ventilation system to eliminate the hazards posed by diesel exhaust.[22]

By the time of the St. Clair Tunnel's 75th anniversary in 1966, the limitations of its 19 foot 10 inch internal width to accommodate changes in rail traffic practices were becoming readily apparent. During this same timeframe came the introduction of taller and longer rail cars optimized for the automotive industry that could not pass through the size restrictions imposed by the tunnel's design. As that sector of industry accounted for a large percentage of the volume of goods passing through the Port Huron-Sarnia corridor on an annual basis, Canadian National had little choice but to establish a ferry service to handle this traffic and the subsequent introduction of double-decked container cars. With regular traffic still passing through the tunnel, the railroad inaugurated service across the St. Clair River for oversized railcars with the tug *Phyllis Yorke* and the barge *St. Clair* in March of 1971. To meet the growing demand, Canadian National added the *Margaret Yorke* and barge *Scotia II* to the route just a few years later.

While the ferries proved themselves a practical solution to the difficulties faced by railroad managers tasked with moving outsized and hazardous freight cars through the border crossing, it nonetheless created the same set of circumstances that led to the construction of the tunnel in the first place. Faced with this dilemma, and having decided against widening the St. Clair Tunnel, Canadian National embarked upon building a new tunnel adjacent to the north side of the existing crossing. Championed by company president Paul M. Tellier, this structure's 27 foot 6 inch internal diameter would accommodate the oversized railcars unable to use the 1891 tunnel. Unlike the first tunnel, which incorporated two tunneling shields working towards each other from opposite sides of the river, this project only involved one tunneling machine that crossed under the St. Clair River to Port Huron from Sarnia. With construction beginning in 1993, the new tunnel opened to rail traffic two years later. Rendered obsolete, workers removed the tracks leading to original tunnel and sealed each of its entrances a short time later. As had taken place just over one-hundred years earlier, the opening of the new tunnel also heralded the end of the railroad's car ferry service across the St. Clair River. Originally given the same name as its predecessor, the 1995 St. Clair Tunnel was subsequently renamed the Paul M. Tellier Tunnel in 2004.

NOTES

Chapter One
An Inferno on Woodward Avenue - 1894

1. Robert B. Ross & George B. Catlin. *Landmarks of Wayne County and Detroit* (Detroit: The Evening News Association, 1898), p. 476.
2. The Weekly Wisconsin, October 13, 1894.
3. *Ibid.*
4. Robert B. Ross & George B. Catlin. *Landmarks of Wayne County and Detroit* (Detroit: The Evening News Association, 1898), p. 476.
5. *Ibid*, p. 476.
6. *Ibid*, p. 476.
7. The Weekly Wisconsin, October 13, 1894.
8. *Ibid.*
9. A pipeman is a fire fighter stationed on the nozzle of a hose.
10. The Weekly Wisconsin, October 13, 1894.
11. The Fort Wayne News, October 5, 1894.
12. Robert B. Ross & George B. Catlin. *Landmarks of Wayne County and Detroit* (Detroit: The Evening News Association, 1898), p. 476.
13. Mount Elliot Cemetery Association. *Mt. Elliot Cemetery: A History* (Detroit: The Mount Elliot Cemetery Association), p. 48.
14. The Fort Wayne Journal-Gazette, March 5, 1917.
15. U.S. Fire Administration. *Technical Report Series: Detroit Warehouse Fire Claims Three Fire Fighters, Detroit, Michigan, USFA-TR-003/March 1987.* (Emmitsburg, Maryland.: U.S. Fire Administration, 1987), p. 1.

Chapter Two
Michigan's Fish Cars – 1888-1938

1. Michigan Department of Natural Resources. *Michigan Fisheries Centennial Report 1873-1973*, p. 4, 20.
2. Michigan Fish Commission. *First Report of the State Commissioners and Superintendent on State Fisheries for 1873-4*, p. 5-6.

Notes

3. Michigan Fish Commission. *Twelfth Biennial Report of the State Board of Fish Commissioners*, p. 8.
4. Michigan Department of Natural Resources. *Michigan Fisheries Centennial Report 1873-1973*, p. 19-20.
5. Michigan Fish Commission. *Second Report of the State Commissioners and Superintendent on State Fisheries for 1875-6*, p. 44.
6. Michigan Department of Natural Resources. *Michigan Fisheries Centennial Report 1873-1973*, p. 25.
7. Michigan Fish Commission. *Eighth Biennial Report of the State Board of Fish Commissioners*, p. 64.
8. *Ibid*, p. 65.
9. *Ibid*, p. 65.
10. *Ibid*, p. 65.
11. Michigan Department of Natural Resources. *Michigan Fisheries Centennial Report 1873-1973*, p. 22.
12. Michigan Fish Commission. *Eighth Biennial Report of the State Board of Fish Commissioners*, p. 65.
13. Michigan Department of Natural Resources. *Michigan Fisheries Centennial Report 1873-1973*, p. 22.
14. Michigan Fish Commission. *Eighth Biennial Report of the State Board of Fish Commissioners*, p. 66.
15. Michigan Fish Commission. *Ninth Biennial Report of the State Board of Fish Commissioners*, p. 39-40.
16. *Ibid*, p. 39.
17. *Ibid*, p. 39.
18. *Ibid*, p. 39.
19. Michigan Fish Commission. *Twelfth Biennial Report of the State Board of Fish Commissioners*, p. 47.
20. *Ibid*, p. 47.
21. Michigan Department of Natural Resources. *Michigan Fisheries Centennial Report 1873-1973*, p. 22.
22. Michigan Fish Commission. *Twenty-First Biennial Report of the State Board of Fish Commissioners*, p. 7-8.
23. Leah Rosenow. *Badger #2 and the Fish Car Era,* Mid-Continent Railway Gazette, Vol. 39, No. 4, p. 12.

24. Michigan Fish Commission. *Twenty-First Biennial Report of the State Board of Fish Commissioners*, p. 7-8.
25. *Ibid*, p. 7. (Note: This report contains an error concerning the length of the *Attikumaig*)
26. Michigan Department of Natural Resources. *Michigan Fisheries Centennial Report* 1873-1973, p. 23.
27. *Ibid*, p. 23.
28. *Ibid*, p. 24.

Chapter Three
Stout Air Services 1926-1930

1. The Ludington Sunday Morning News, August 1, 1926.
2. Detroit-Grand Rapids Airline. *December 1, 1926 Timetable*.
3. Robert F. Pauley. *Michigan Aircraft Manufacturers*. (Mount Pleasant, South Carolina: Arcadia Publishing), p. 30.
4. Kenneth Munson. *U.S. Commercial Aircraft*. (London: Jane's Publishing Company Limited, 1982.), p. 19.
5. *Ibid*, p. 19.
6. Detroit-Grand Rapids Airline. *December 1, 1926 Timetable*.
7. Stout Air Lines. *July 15, 1929 Timetable*.
8. Detroit-Grand Rapids Airline. *March 1, 1927 Timetable*.
9. Detroit-Cleveland Airline. *April 1, 1928 Timetable*.
10. The Escanaba Daily News, July 28, 1927.
11. *Ibid*.
12. Detroit-Cleveland Airline. *April 1, 1928 Timetable*.
13. *Ibid*.
14. The Billings Gazette, April 29, 1929.
15. *Ibid*.
16. Stout Air Services. *Stout Air Lines Detroit-Cleveland-Chicago July 15, 1929 Timetable*.
17. Marshall Evening Chronicle, December 11, 1929.
18. Stout Air Lines. *January 2, 1930 Timetable*.
19. San Antonio Sunday Light, September 21, 1930.
20. Oakland Tribune, September 21, 1930.
21. The Tipton Daily Tribune, November 19, 1930.

22. The Ludington Daily News, November 25, 1930.
23. The Oakland Tribune, December 24, 1930.

Chapter Four
A Simple Misunderstanding - 1905

1. The Mining Gazette, April 17, 1905.
2. *Ibid.*
3. *Ibid.*
4. The La Crosse Tribune, April 17, 1905. *[Note: If Daniel Hardiman did in fact perform this feat, then history has dealt the bridge engineer a significant injustice.]*
5. The Mining Gazette, April 17, 1905.
6. U.S. House of Representatives. *Reports of the Department of Commerce and Labor - 1906*, p. 382.
7. War Department. *Annual Reports of the War Department for the Fiscal Year Ended June 30, 1905, Volume VI, Report of the Chief of Engineers*, p. 1998.
8. John T. Gaertner. *Duluth, South Shore & Atlantic Railway, p. 157-158.*
9. John O. Greenwood. *Namesakes 1910-1919*, p. 204.
10. J. B. Mansfield. *History of the Great Lakes Vol. I*, p. 457.
11. Julius F. Wolf Jr. Lake Superior Shipwrecks, p. 95.
12. John O. Greenwood. *Namesakes 1910-1919*, p. 204.

Chapter Five
Captain Curtis Boughton – 1813-1896

1. The News-Palladium, December 31, 1946.
2. Franklin Ellis. *History of Berrien and Van Buren Counties, Michigan.* (Philadelphia, Pennsylvania: D. W. Ensign & Co., 1880), p. 313.
3. The News-Palladium, December 31, 1946.

4. Franklin Ellis. *History of Berrien and Van Buren Counties, Michigan.* (Philadelphia, Pennsylvania: D. W. Ensign & Co., 1880), p. 41.
5. Southport Telegraph, November 30, 1842.
6. James Pender. *History of Benton Harbor and Tales of Village Days.* (Chicago, Illinois: The Braun Printing Co., 1915), p. 159.
7. Franklin Ellis. *History of Berrien and Van Buren Counties, Michigan.* (Philadelphia, Pennsylvania: D. W. Ensign & Co., 1880), p. 122.
8. Orville W. Coolidge. *A Twentieth Century History of Berrien County Michigan.* (Chicago, Illinois: The Lewis Publishing Company, 1906), p. 56.
9. The News-Palladium, December 31, 1946.
10. James Pender. *History of Benton Harbor and Tales of Village Days.* (Chicago, Illinois: The Braun Printing Co., 1915), p. 159.
11. The News-Palladium, December 31, 1946.
12. James Pender. *History of Benton Harbor and Tales of Village Days.* (Chicago, Illinois: The Braun Printing Co., 1915), p. 10.
13. Saint Joseph Herald, September 19, 1868.
14. Franklin Ellis. *History of Berrien and Van Buren Counties, Michigan.* (Philadelphia, Pennsylvania: D. W. Ensign & Co., 1880), p. 55-56.
15. The News-Palladium, December 31, 1946.

Chapter Six
Tragic Oversight – 1926

1. Although many newspaper accounts of the accident relate the motorman's name as Willis Owens, the official Interstate Commerce Commission report, along with several subsequent news articles published during the following months, list his name as Willis Owen.
2. Nicholas, Frederic (Editor). *American Street Railway Investments.* (New York City: McGraw Publishing Company, 1910), p. 155-156.
3. Street Railway Journal. "Completion of the Interurban Line Between Toledo and Detroit," *Street Railway Journal, Volume 25 No. 4, January 28, 1905.* (New York City: McGraw Publishing Company, 1905), p. 144.

4. Interstate Commerce Commission. *Report of the Director of the Bureau of Safety in Re: Investigation of an Accident which Occurred on the Detroit, Monroe & Toledo Short Line Railway, Detroit United Lines, Near Monroe, Mich., on September 2, 1926.* (Washington D.C.: Interstate Commerce Commission, 1926), p. 2-3.

5. *Ibid.*, p. 2-3.

6. *Ibid.*, p. 2-3.

7. *Ibid.*, p. 1.

8. *Ibid.*, p. 3.

9. The Times Recorder, September 3, 1926.

10. Ludington Daily News, September 3, 1926.

11. Traverse City Record, September 4, 1926.

12. Interstate Commerce Commission. *Report of the Director of the Bureau of Safety in Re: Investigation of an Accident which Occurred on the Detroit, Monroe & Toledo Short Line Railway, Detroit United Lines, Near Monroe, Mich., on September 2, 1926.* (Washington D.C.: Interstate Commerce Commission, 1926), p. 2-3.

13. *Ibid.*, p. 3; The Ludington Daily News, October 8, 1926.

14. *Ibid.*, p. 4.

Chapter Seven
Alpena's Great Fire of 1872

1. David D. Oliver. *Centennial History of Alpena County, Michigan.* (Alpena, Michigan: Argus Printing House, 1903), p. 28.

2. *Ibid.*, p. 49.

3. Perry F. Powers. *A History of Northern Michigan and its People, Volume I.* (Chicago, Illinois: The Lewis Publishing Company, 1912), p. 465.

4. David D. Oliver. *Centennial History of Alpena County, Michigan.* (Alpena, Michigan: Argus Printing House, 1903), p. 49 & 62.

5. Perry F. Powers. *A History of Northern Michigan and its People, Volume I.* (Chicago, Illinois: The Lewis Publishing Company, 1912), p. 467.

6. *Ibid.*, p. 469.

7. David D. Oliver. *Centennial History of Alpena County, Michigan.* (Alpena, Michigan: Argus Printing House, 1903), p. 122.

8. *Ibid.*, p. 128-129.

9. *Ibid.*, p. 128-131.
10. *Ibid.*, p. 131-132.
11. *Ibid.*, p. 132.
12. The Daily Gazette, July 15, 1872.
13. The Evansville Daily Courier, July 14, 1872.
14. David D. Oliver. *Centennial History of Alpena County, Michigan.* (Alpena, Michigan: Argus Printing House, 1903), p. 92, 127, 166.
15. The Daily Gazette, July 15, 1872.
16. William S. Boulton. *Alpena County, Pioneer Collections, Report of the Pioneer Society of the State of Michigan, Volume VI.* (Lansing, Michigan: W.S. George & Co., State Printers and Binders, 1884), p. 186.
17. *Ibid.*, p. 186.
18. A fire limit is a section of a city in which buildings must be made of brick rather than wood to prevent devastating fires.
19. David D. Oliver. *Centennial History of Alpena County, Michigan.* (Alpena, Michigan: Argus Printing House, 1903), p. 124, 135.
20. Columbus Daily Herald, July 13, 1888.

Chapter Eight
The Balkan Mine Disaster - 1914

1. George J. Miller. *"Some Geographic Influences of the Lake Superior Iron Ores."* (New York: Bulletin of the American Geographical Society Volume 46 Number 12, 1914), p. 884.
2. Walter Havighurst. *Vein of Iron.* (Cleveland, Ohio: The World Publishing Company, 1958), p. 107-108.
3. *Mining Press Vol. 109, July to December 1914*, p. 306
4. The Ironwood Times, July 18, 1914.
5. *Mining Press Vol. 109, July to December 1914*, p. 306
6. The Ironwood Times, July 18, 1914.
7. Manitowoc Daily Herald, July 15, 1914.
8. Newspaper reports published at the time of the accident contain a number of spelling differences for the last names of the victims. The information listed here is from the July 18, 1914 edition of *The Ironwood Times*.
9. Manitowoc Daily Herald, July 15, 1914.

10. The newspaper reported Antonio Boschi's surname as Boscele.

11. Walter Havighurst. *Vein of Iron*. (Cleveland, Ohio: The World Publishing Company, 1958), p. 108.

Chapter Nine
Cholera Epidemic at Detroit – 1832

1. Robert B. Ross & George B. Catlin. *Landmarks of Wayne County and Detroit* (Detroit: The Evening News Association, 1898), p. 380.

2. Burton, Clarence M. *The City of Detroit, Michigan, 1702-1922, Volume 2* (Detroit: The S. J. Clarke Publishing Company, 1922), p. 1055.

3. The Frederick Herald, July 28, 1832.

4. Burton, Clarence M. *The City of Detroit, Michigan, 1702-1922, Volume 2* (Detroit: The S. J. Clarke Publishing Company, 1922), p. 1055.

5. *Ibid.*, p. 1212-1215.

6. Farmer, Silas. *History of Detroit and Wayne County and Early Michigan, Third Edition* (New York: Munsell & Co., 1890), p. 531.

7. *Ibid.*, p. 531.

8. Adams Sentinel, September 7, 1832.

9. Robert B. Ross & George B. Catlin. *Landmarks of Wayne County and Detroit* (Detroit: The Evening News Association, 1898), p. 381-383.

Chapter Ten
Dog Sled Teams of the Upper Peninsula

1. Joseph M. Mayer. *Canals Between the Lakes and New York, American Society of Civil Engineers, Transactions No. 889.* (New York: American Society of Civil Engineers, 1901), p. 293.

2. Edward F. Watrous. *Dog Teams and Sledges in Michigan, St. Nicholas Illustrated Magazine, Volume 28.* (New York: The Century Co., 1901), p. 346.

3. *Ibid.*, p. 347-349.

4. Some sources refer to Antoine Paquette as Antoine Piquette.

5. Caspar Whitney (Editor). *The Dog Teams of the "Soo," The Outing Magazine, Volume 52, April-September 1908.* (New York: The Outing Publishing Company, 1908), p. 334.
6. Caspar Whitney (Editor). *John Boucher-Rapids Pilot, The Outing Magazine, Volume 46, April-September 1905.* (New York: The Outing Publishing Company, 1905), p. 478.
7. Caspar Whitney (Editor). *The Dog Teams of the "Soo," The Outing Magazine, Volume 52, April-September 1908.* (New York: The Outing Publishing Company, 1908), p. 333.
8. The Evening News, March 19, 1970.
9. Caspar Whitney (Editor). *The Dog Teams of the "Soo," The Outing Magazine, Volume 52, April-September 1908.* (New York: The Outing Publishing Company, 1908), p. 334.
10. Wisconsin Rapids Daily Tribune, March 12, 1928.
11. The Capital Times, March 16, 1928.
12. *Ibid.*
13. The Ironwood Daily Globe, March 21, 1928.

Chapter Eleven
Grand Rapids Tornado - 1912

1. Albert Baxter. *History of the City of Grand Rapids, Michigan* (New York: Munsell & Company, 1891), p. 89.
2. The Fort Wayne Sentinel, July 17, 1912; The Daily Reflector, July 16, 1912; The News Palladium, July 13, 1912.
3. The Daily Reflector, July 16, 1912.
4. The Evening Herald, July 13, 1912.
5. The Fort Wayne Sentinel, July 17, 1912.
6. The Daily Reflector, July 16, 1912.
7. The Syracuse Herald, July 13, 1912.

Chapter Twelve
Deadly Windfall

1. John O. Greenwood. *Fleet Histories, Volume Two.* (Cleveland, Ohio: Freshwater Press Inc., 1992), p. 46.

2. Some references identify the *Boyd*'s captain as M. W. Whitney or W.M Whitney. The name used here appears in subsequent press reports concerning the official investigation of the wreck.

3. The Star Journal, November 10, 1936.

4. The Evening News, November 9, 1936.

5. *Ibid.*

6. The Evening News, November 10, 1936.

7. *Ibid.*

8. The Evening News, November 11, 1936.

9. The Evening News, November 10, 1936.

10. John O. Greenwood. *Fleet Histories, Volume Two.* (Cleveland, Ohio: Freshwater Press Inc., 1992), p. 46.

11. The Hammond Times, November 12, 1936.

12. The Evening News, November 11, 1936.

13. John O. Greenwood. *Fleet Histories, Volume Two.* (Cleveland, Ohio: Freshwater Press Inc., 1992), p. 46.

14. The Evening News, November 13, 1936; The Evening News, November 14, 1936.

15. Appleton Post-Crescent, January 2, 1937.

16. Automobile Topics. "Wills Gets Out in Time." *Automobile Topics, Volume 63, No. 6, September 24, 1921.* (New York City: Automobile Topics, 1921), p. 442.

17. The Oshkosh Northwestern, January 2, 1937.

18. *Ibid.*

19. Appleton Post-Crescent, January 2, 1937.

20. The Oshkosh Northwestern, January 2, 1937; Appleton Post-Crescent, January 2, 1937.

21. Appleton Post-Crescent, January 4, 1937.

22. Benjamin J. Shelak. *Shipwrecks of Lake Michigan.* (Black Earth, Wisconsin: Trails Books, 2003), p. 163.

23. The Sheboygan Press, March 1, 1937.

24. The Evening News, March 3, 1937.

25. The Sheboygan Press, March 1, 1937.

26. The Evening News, March 2, 1937.

27. Ironwood Daily Globe, June 15, 1937.

28. *The J. Oswald Boyd, No. 15880.* 53 F.Supp. 103 (1943) United States District Court, Eastern District, Michigan, December 21, 1943.

29. Ironwood Daily Globe, July 16, 1942.
30. *The J. Oswald Boyd, No. 15880.* 53 F.Supp. 103 (1943) United States District Court, Eastern District, Michigan, December 21, 1943.
31. Ironwood Daily Globe, July 16, 1942.

Chapter Thirteen
Disaster on Easter Sunday – 1958

1. The News-Palladium, September 20, 1943.
2. Although fitted with propellers, a turboprop aircraft incorporates turbine engines in contrast to other propeller driven types equipped with reciprocating powerplants.
3. Civil Aeronautics Board. *Aircraft Accident Report, Capital Airlines, Inc., Viscount, Tri-City Airport, Freeland, Michigan, April 6, 1958 , Revised 1965* (Washington D.C.: Civil Aeronautics Board, 1965), p. 17.
4. For the purposes of clarity, all times for April 6, 1958 are expressed in Central Standard Time.
5. Civil Aeronautics Board. *Aircraft Accident Report, Capital Airlines, Inc., Viscount, Tri-City Airport, Freeland, Michigan, April 6, 1958 , Revised 1965* (Washington D.C.: Civil Aeronautics Board, 1965), p. 2 -3.
6. The News-Palladium, April 7, 1958.
7. *Ibid.*
8. Some references list Ruth M. Denecke as being from St. Petersburg, Florida.
9. The Holland Evening Sentinel, April 8, 1958.
10. The Civil Aeronautics Board relinquished its aviation accident investigation duties to the National Transportation Safety Board (NTSB) in 1967 prior to its complete disbandment on December 31, 1984.
11. Civil Aeronautics Board. *Aircraft Accident Report, Capital Airlines, Inc., Viscount, Tri-City Airport, Freeland, Michigan, April 6, 1958 , Revised 1965.* (Washington D.C.: Civil Aeronautics Board, 1965), p. 3.
12. *Ibid.*, p. 12.
13. *Ibid.*, p. 6.

14. The News-Palladium, July 10, 1958.
15. The Ludington Daily News, June 4, 1958.
16. Civil Aeronautics Board. *Aircraft Accident Report, Capital Airlines, Inc., Viscount, Tri-City Airport, Freeland, Michigan, April 6, 1958, Revised 1965.* (Washington D.C.: Civil Aeronautics Board, 1965), p. 7-8.
17. International Civil Aviation Organization. *ICAO Circular, Aircraft Accident Digest No. 10, Circular 59-AN/54.* (Montreal, Canada: International Civil Aviation Organization, 1961), p. 117.
18. Civil Aeronautics Board. *Aircraft Accident Report, Continental Airlines, Inc., Vickers Viscount 812, N242V, Municipal Airport, Kansas City, Missouri, January 29, 1963.* (Washington D.C.: Civil Aeronautics Board, 1964), p. 13.
19. Civil Aeronautics Board. *Aircraft Accident Report, Capital Airlines, Inc., Viscount, Tri-City Airport, Freeland, Michigan, April 6, 1958, Revised 1965.* (Washington D.C.: Civil Aeronautics Board, 1965), p. 10-11, 16.

Chapter Fourteen
Abraham Lincoln Visits Kalamazoo – 1856

1. Another variation of this slogan was, "Free speech, free press, free soil, free men, Frémont and victory!"
2. Thomas I. Starr. *Lincoln's Kalamazoo Address Against Extending Slavery.* (Detroit: Fine Book Circle, 1941), p. 13.
3. Daily Hawk-Eye & Telegraph, August 30, 1856.
4. Thomas I. Starr. *Lincoln's Kalamazoo Address Against Extending Slavery.* (Detroit: Fine Book Circle, 1941), p. 11-12.
5. Daily Hawk-Eye & Telegraph, August 30, 1856.
6. Thomas I. Starr. *Lincoln's Kalamazoo Address Against Extending Slavery.* (Detroit: Fine Book Circle, 1941), p. 23.
7. *Ibid.*, p. 18, 23.
8. *Ibid.*, p. 12, 23- 24.
9. *Ibid.*, p. 10.
10. *Ibid.*, p. 18.

Chapter Fifteen
The St. Clair Tunnel – 1891

1. Hilton, George W. *The Great Lakes Car Ferries*. (Berkeley, California: Howell-North Books, 1962), p. 12-13.
2. National Park Service. *Historic American Engineering Record: St. Clair Tunnel (St. Clair River Tunnel), HAER No. MI-67*. (Philadelphia, Pennsylvania: National Park Service, 1993), p. 5.
3. *Ibid.*, p. 2.
4. *Ibid.*, p. 8.
5. In terms of mining, a drift is defined as a horizontal or inclined passage.
6. National Park Service. *Historic American Engineering Record: St. Clair Tunnel (St. Clair River Tunnel), HAER No. MI-67*. (Philadelphia, Pennsylvania: National Park Service, 1993), p. 9.
7. Spelled by some sources as "tunnelling shield."
8. The Statesman, September 25, 1891.
9. National Park Service. *Historic American Engineering Record: St. Clair Tunnel (St. Clair River Tunnel), HAER No. MI-67*. (Philadelphia, Pennsylvania: National Park Service, 1993), p. 14-15; The Statesman, September 25, 1891.
10. National Park Service. *Historic American Engineering Record: St. Clair Tunnel (St. Clair River Tunnel), HAER No. MI-67*. (Philadelphia, Pennsylvania: National Park Service, 1993), p. 18; The Statesman, September 25, 1891.
11. National Park Service. *Historic American Engineering Record: St. Clair Tunnel (St. Clair River Tunnel), HAER No. MI-67*. (Philadelphia, Pennsylvania: National Park Service, 1993), p. 16-17.
12. *Ibid.*, p. 25.
13. National Park Service. *Historic American Engineering Record: St. Clair Tunnel (St. Clair River Tunnel), HAER No. MI-67*. (Philadelphia, Pennsylvania: National Park Service, 1993), p. 28; The Statesman, September 25, 1891.
14. National Park Service. *Historic American Engineering Record: St. Clair Tunnel (St. Clair River Tunnel), HAER No. MI-67*. (Philadelphia, Pennsylvania: National Park Service, 1993), p. 27-28.

Notes

15. Sager, F. A. & Arnold, Bion J. *Electrification of the St. Clair Tunnel.* (Montreal, Quebec: Grand Trunk Railway System, 1908), p. 10.
16. National Park Service. *Historic American Engineering Record: St. Clair Tunnel (St. Clair River Tunnel), HAER No. MI-67.* (Philadelphia, Pennsylvania: National Park Service, 1993), p. 29.
17. *Ibid.*, p. 30.
18. National Park Service. *Historic American Engineering Record: St. Clair Tunnel (St. Clair River Tunnel), HAER No. MI-67.* (Philadelphia, Pennsylvania: National Park Service, 1993), p. 31; Sager, F. A. & Arnold, Bion J. *Electrification of the St. Clair Tunnel.* (Montreal, Quebec: Grand Trunk Railway System, 1908), p. 10-11, 21 -22.
19. National Park Service. *Historic American Engineering Record: St. Clair Tunnel (St. Clair River Tunnel), HAER No. MI-67.* (Philadelphia, Pennsylvania: National Park Service, 1993), p. 31-32 ; Sager, F. A. & Arnold, Bion J. *Electrification of the St. Clair Tunnel.* (Montreal, Quebec: Grand Trunk Railway System, 1908), p. 5, 12, 15.
20. Chardavoyne, David G. *The United States District Court for the Eastern District of Michigan. People, Law, and Politics.* (Detroit, Michigan: Wayne State University Press, 2012), p. 159-161; The Mansfield News, December 22, 1917.
21. National Park Service. *Historic American Engineering Record: St. Clair Tunnel (St. Clair River Tunnel), HAER No. MI-67.* (Philadelphia, Pennsylvania: National Park Service, 1993), p. 33; The News-Palladium, June 17, 1940.
22. National Park Service. *Historic American Engineering Record: St. Clair Tunnel (St. Clair River Tunnel), HAER No. MI-67.* (Philadelphia, Pennsylvania: National Park Service, 1993), p. 33; Gilbert, Clare. *St. Clair River Tunnel: Rails Beneath the River.* (Erin, Ontario: Boston Mills Press, 1991), p. 64.

BIBLIOGRAPHY

Baxter, Albert. *History of the City of Grand Rapids, Michigan.* New York City, New York: Munsell & Company Publishers, 1891.

Boulton, William S. *Alpena County, Pioneer Collections, Report of the Pioneer Society of the State of Michigan, Volume VI.* Lansing, Michigan: W.S. George & Co., State Printers and Binders, 1884.

Burton, Clarence M. (Editor). *The City of Detroit 1702-1922, Volume 2.* Detroit, Michigan: The S. J. Clarke Publishing Company, 1922.

Chardavoyne, David G. *The United States District Court for the Eastern District of Michigan. People, Law, and Politics.* Detroit, Michigan: Wayne State University Press, 2012.

Civil Aeronautics Board. *Aircraft Accident Report, Capital Airlines, Inc., Viscount, Tri-City Airport, Freeland, Michigan, April 6, 1958, Revised 1965.* Washington D.C.: Civil Aeronautics Board, 1965.

————. *Aircraft Accident Report, Continental Airlines, Inc., Vickers Viscount 812, N242V, Municipal Airport, Kansas City, Missouri, January 29, 1963.* Washington D.C.: Civil Aeronautics Board, 1964.

Coolidge, Orville W. *A Twentieth Century History of Berrien County Michigan.* Chicago, Illinois: The Lewis Publishing Company, 1906.

Ellis, Franklin. *History of Berrien and Van Buren Counties.* Philadelphia, Pennsylvania: D. W. Ensign & Co., 1880.

Farmer, Silas. *History of Detroit and Wayne County and Early Michigan, Third Edition.* New York City, New York: Munsell & Co., 1890.

Gaertner, John. *Duluth, South Shore & Atlantic Railway.* Bloomington, Indiana: Indiana University Press, 2008.

Gilbert, Clare. *St. Clair River Tunnel: Rails Beneath the River.* Erin, Ontario: Boston Mills Press, 1991.

Greenwood, John O. *Namesakes 1910-1919.* Cleveland, Ohio: Freshwater Press, Inc., 1986.

Bibliography

————. *The Fleet Histories Series, Volume Two.* Cleveland, Ohio: Freshwater Press, Inc., 1992.

Havighurst, Walter. *Vein of Iron.* Cleveland, Ohio: The World Publishing Company, 1958.

Hilton, George W. *The Great Lakes Car Ferries.* Berkeley, California: Howell-North Books, 1962.

International Civil Aviation Organization. *ICAO Circular, Aircraft Accident Digest No. 10, Circular 59-AN/54.* Montreal, Canada: International Civil Aviation Organization, 1961.

Interstate Commerce Commission. *Report of the Director of the Bureau of Safety in RE Investigation of an Accident which Occurred on the Detroit, Monroe & Toledo Short Line Railway, Detroit United Lines, Near Monroe, Mich., on September 2, 1926.* Washington D.C.: Interstate Commerce Commission, 1926.

Mansfield, J. B. *History of the Great Lakes, Volume I.* Chicago, Illinois: J. H. Beers & Co., 1899.

Michigan Department of Natural Resources. *Michigan Fisheries Centennial Report 1873-1973.* Lansing, Michigan: Department of Natural Resources, 1973.

Michigan Fish Commission. *Eighth Biennial Report of the State Board of Fish Commissioners.* Lansing, Michigan: Darius D. Thorp, State Printer and Binder, 1889.

————. *First Report of the State Commissioners and Superintendent on State Fisheries for 1873-4.* Lansing, Michigan: W.S. George & Co., State Printers and Binders, 1875.

————. *Ninth Biennial Report of the State Board of Fish Commissioners.* Lansing, Michigan: Robert Smith Printing Co., State Printers and Binders, 1890.

————. *Second Report of the State Commissioners and Superintendent on State Fisheries for 1875-6.* Lansing, Michigan: W.S. George & Co., State Printers and Binders, 1876.

————. *Twelfth Biennial Report of the State Board of Fish Commissioners*. Lansing, Michigan: Robert Smith Printing Co., State Printers and Binders, 1897.

————. *Twenty-First Biennial Report of the State Board of Fish Commissioners*. Lansing, Michigan: Wynkoop Hallenbeck Crawford Co., State Printers, 1915.

Michigan State Pioneer Society. *Pioneer Collections, Report of the Pioneer Society of the State of Michigan, Vol. IV.* Lansing, Michigan: W. S. George & Co. Printers and Binders, 1888.

Miller, George J. *"Some Geographic Influences of the Lake Superior Iron Ores." Bulletin of the American Geographical Society Volume 46.* New York City, New York: American Geographical Society, 1914.

Mt Elliot Cemetery Association. *Mt. Elliot Cemetery: A History.* Detroit, Michigan: Mt. Elliot Cemetery Association.

Munson, Kenneth. *U.S. Commercial Aircraft.* London, England: Jane's Publishing Company, Ltd., 1982.

National Park Service. *Historic American Engineering Record: St. Clair Tunnel (St. Clair River Tunnel), HAER No. MI-67.* Philadelphia, Pennsylvania: National Park Service, 1993.

Nicholas, Frederic (Editor). *American Street Railway Investments.* New York City, New York: McGraw Publishing Company, 1910.

Oliver, David D. *Centennial History of Alpena County Michigan.* Alpena, Michigan: Argus Printing House, 1903.

Pauley, Robert F. *Images of America: Michigan Aircraft Manufacturers.* Mount Pleasant, South Carolina: Arcadia Publishing, 2009.

Pender, James. *History of Benton Harbor and Tales of Village Days.* Chicago, Illinois: The Braun Printing Company, 1915.

Periodical Publishing Co. *The Grand Rapids Furniture Record.* Grand Rapids, Michigan: Periodical Publishing Co., 1919.

Bibliography

Powers, Perry F. *A History of Northern Michigan and its People, Volume I.* Chicago, Illinois: The Lewis Publishing Company, 1912.

R. L. Polk & Co. *Detroit City Directory 1895.* Detroit, Michigan: R. L. Polk & Co., 1895.

Ratigan, William. *Great Lakes Shipwrecks and Survivals.* Grand Haven, Michigan: Wm. B. Eerdmans Publishing Co., 1977.

Rosenow, Leah. *Badger #2 and the Fish Car Era. Mid-Continent Railway Gazette, Vol. 39 No. 4, December 2006.* North Freedom, Wisconsin: Mid-Continent Railway Museum, 2006.

Ross, Robert B. & Catlin, George B. *Landmarks of Wayne County and Detroit.* Detroit, Michigan: The Evening News Association, 1898.

Sager, F. A. & Arnold, Bion J. *Electrification of the St. Clair Tunnel.* Montreal, Quebec: Grand Trunk Railway System, 1908.

Shelak, Benjamin J. *Shipwrecks of Lake Michigan.* Black Earth, Wisconsin: Trails Books, 2003.

Stevens, Deidre. *Images of America: Sault Ste. Marie.* Mount Pleasant, South Carolina: Arcadia Publishing, 2008.

Stout, William B. *So Away I went!* Indianapolis, Indiana: Bobb-Merril, 1951.

Thomopoulos, Elaine Cotsirilos. *Images of America: St. Joseph and Benton Harbor.* Mount Pleasant, South Carolina: Arcadia Publishing, 2004.

U.S. Fire Administration. *Technical Report Series: Detroit Warehouse Fire Claims Three Fire Fighters, Detroit, Michigan, USFA-TR-003/March 1987.* Emmitsburg, Maryland: U.S. Fire Administration.

U.S. Navy Hydrographic Office. *Notice to Mariners No. 17, April 29, 1905.* Washington D.C.: U.S. Navy Bureau of Equipment, 1905.

Wolf, Julius F., Jr. *Lake Superior Shipwrecks.* Duluth, Minnesota: Lake Superior Port Cities, Inc., 1990.

INDEX

2-AT Air Pullman, aircraft, 18-21, 23
3-AT, aircraft, 23

A. Auspach's Dry Goods Store, 53
A. Herr's Furniture Store, 53
A. L. Power & Co. Grocery Store, 53
Adams, Homer, 42-49
Alaska, 67
Albany, New York, 60
Alpena, Michigan, founding of, 50-51;
    lumber industry, 51; economic
    growth of, 51-52; financial
    institutions, 52; early fires, 52;
    organization of fire department, 52;
    1872 fire, 53-55; new fire
    regulations and rebuilding of, 55.
Alpena Banking Co., 52
Alpena County, Michigan, 51, 54
Alpena Weekly Argus, newspaper, 54
Alpha, Michigan, 57, 59
American Party, 102
American Ship Building Company, 34
Arkansas, 76
Attikumaig, fish car, 12-14

B-24 Liberator, aircraft, 91
Bagley, John J., 7
Baldwin Locomotive Works, 118, 120
Balkan Mine, opening of, 57; flooding
    of, 58; bodies recovered from, 59;
    reopening of, 59.
Balkan Mining Company, 57
Bancroft, schooner, 36
Batesta, Rossi, 59
Bath, New York, 35
Battan, Batista, 58-59
Battle Creek, Michigan, 26
Battle Creek Glee Club, 104

Bay City, Michigan, 91, 95, 100
Beatty, Joseph, 88
Beaver Island, 79-80, 82-84
Beaver Island Transit Company, 83,
    86
Begg, Alexander S., 120
Belle Isle, 61
Benton Harbor, Michigan, 35, 37-39
Berrien County, Michigan, 8, 35, 38
Bevola, Dominco, 58
Big Rapids, Michigan, 38
Bingham, Kinsley S., 103
Binkley, Earle M., 92-93, 95
Bishop Airport, 92
Black Hawk, Sauk warrior, 60
Black Hawk War, 60-61
Blaiklock, M. S., 116
Blissfield, Michigan, 46
Blue Water Bridge, 110
Boggs, Samuel, 52
Boschi, Antonio, 58-59
Boucher, John, 68-69
Boughton, Curtis, birth of, 35; sailing
    career, 35; relocation to Berrien
    County, 35; marriage and children,
    36; salvage of the *Pioneer*, 35;
    acquisition of schooners, 36;
    shipping of peaches to Chicago,
    36-37; further business pursuits,
    37-39; death of, 39
Boughton, James, 36
Boughton, John, 36
Bow, McLachlan & Company
    Limited, 78
Bower, Seymour, 14
Breakenridge, E. A., 50
Breen Mine, 56
Breitung, Edward N., 57

Index

Brevort, Michigan, 85-86
British Admiralty, 78
Bronson Park, 102, 104-105, 107
Brooks, Grant, 87
Brown, H. M., 38
Brunson, Allen, 37
Buffalo, New York, 34, 60
Burns, Elizabeth, 46
Burrell House, 53
Burt, William A., 56
Bussey, Fred J., 4

C. C. Whitney's Drug Store, 53
California, 39, 95, 102
Camden, New Jersey, 83
Canada, 105, 110-111, 121
Canadian National Railways, 122-124
Capital Airlines, 92, 94-98, 100
Carringway, Captain, 29, 31
Carter, Daniel, 50-51
Cass County, Michigan, 8
Cedarville, Michigan, 86-87
Central League Baseball Park, 74
Chandler, Zachariah, 103-104
Charlevoix, Michigan, 13-14, 83-84
Chicago, Illinois, 15, 21, 25-27, 35-39,
    57, 60-61, 73, 85, 92, 103-104, 107,
    110, 118
Chicago & West Michigan Railway,
    14
Cholera, 60-62, 64-65
Civil Aeronautics Board, 96-99
Civil War, 37, 50, 106, 108
Clark, George, 7
Clay, Henry, 66
Cleveland, Ohio, 23-24, 26-27, 33, 35,
    90
Cleveland Tankers, 81
Cole, Everett, 83, 84, 86
Cole, Raymond, 84, 86

Continental Airlines, 99
Copper Island, 32
Copper Range Railroad, 33
Court House Square, 107
Crescent City, steamer, 33
Cronin, Bartholomew, 4
Crystal Falls, Michigan, 56-57
Crystal Springs, Michigan, 8
Cummings, Julius G., 3

Dallas, Texas, 26
Daniel Waters Cassard Field, 18
Dayton, William L., 102
DC-3, airliner, 96
De Tour, 70-72, 88-90
Deadman, John F., 71-72
Dearborn, Michigan, 18, 21, 24
Dely, Joseph R., 3
DeMary, Ralph, 31
Democratic Party, 101
Denecke, Ruth M., 95
Detroit, Michigan, 1, 5-6, 8-9, 18-19,
    22-27, 40-43, 46, 52, 60-65, 79, 88-89,
    91-92, 103-104, 115, 121-122
Detroit Chair Company, 5
Detroit Daily Advertiser, newspaper,
    107-108
Detroit Edison Company, 120
Detroit Fire Department, 4, 6
Detroit Glee Club, 104
Detroit River, 9, 79, 89
Detroit United Lines, 40-41
Detroit United Railway, 40
Detroit Wheel & Foundry Company,
    115
Detroit, Monroe & Toledo Short Line
    Railway, formation of, 41;
    operational practices of, 41-42;
    September 2, 1926 accident, 42-49;
    found in violation of federal service

law, 48-49.

Detroit-Cleveland Airline, 24

Detroit-Grand Rapids Airline, formation of, 18; operation of, 18-19; early passenger and freight carriage, 22; suspension of service, 22

Dilhet, John, 63

Donaghue, Michael H., 3

Draheim, Fred, 4

Drift, schooner, 36

Dundee, Michigan, 46

Eagle Hotel, 53

Eau Claire, Wisconsin, 76

Ecorse, Michigan, 7, 41

Elliot, James R., 5

Emig, Oswald, 80

England, 92, 117

Erie Canal, 60

Escanaba, Michigan, 86

Escanaba, cutter, 80, 90

Evergreen Hall, 52

Favorite, tugboat, 80-82, 90

Ferguson, Jack, 46

Field's Cloak & Suit Company, 6

Fillmore, Millard, 102

Fireman's Hall, 107

Fitch, Ben, 46

Fletcher, George N., 50

Flight 67, route of, 92; departure from Newark, 92; crash at Freeland, 93; rescue efforts, 94; identification of victims, 94-95; investigation into crash of, 96-99; revision of initial crash report, 99

Flint, Michigan, 92

Florida Airways, 21

Fontinalis, fish car, 14-15

Ford, Henry, 20, 23

Ford Air Transport Service, 19, 21, 23

Ford Airport, 18, 21, 23-26

Ford Motor Company, 21

Ford Tri-Motor, 19, 23-26

Fort Erie, Ontario, 122

Fort Gratiot, 61

Fort Gratiot, Michigan, 110-111

Foster, J. W., 56

Freeland, Michigan, 91, 96, 99-100

Fremont, Michigan, 50-51

Frémont, John C., 50

French Revolution, 62

General Markham, steamer, 81-82

Genoa, Italy, 34

Germany, 122

Gibbs, Charles, 76

Gibraltar, Michigan, 41

Globe Iron Works, 33

Goetzville, Michigan, 72

Goodrich's Jewelry Store, 53

Gotham Marine Corporation, 78

Grace Hospital, 4

Grand Haven, Michigan, 9, 79-80

Grand Rapids, Michigan, 16, 18-19, 21-22, 38, 73-76

Grand River, 73

Grand Trunk Railway, 110-111, 114, 117-118, 120, 123

Grant Iron and Metal Company, 89

Gray, Michael C., 4

Great Lakes, 7, 24, 34-36, 56, 60, 68, 78-79, 86, 90

Great Lakes Steel Corporation, 89

Great Lakes Towing Company, 80, 90

Great Lakes Transit Company, 34

Great Western Railway, 111

Green Bay, 86

Green, Fred W., 26

Index

Greenland, 90

Gurry, Thomas, 4

Hamilton, Ontario, 115

Hamilton Bridge and Tool Company, 114

Hancock, Michigan, 28, 33

Hardiman, Daniel, 29-31

Hebner, A. W., 46

Heffner, Arthur, 47

Henry Clay, steamer, 60-61

Henry U. King, schooner, 35-36

Herig, Henry, 4

Hertel, George, 47

Hicks, Harold, 23

Higgins, Robert F., 98

Hill, Barbara, 18

Hill, Leon, 84, 86

Hill, Ludlow L., 84, 86

Hill, Robert G., 18

Hillman, Thomas E., 112, 116

Hippocampus, steamer, 37-38

Hitchcock, Samuel E., 54

Hobson, Joseph, 111-118

Hog Island, 61

Holland, Michigan, 38, 96

Hotchkiss, Blue and Company, 15

Houghton, Michigan, 28, 33

Houghton, Douglass, 28

Hoyt, Benjamin C., 35

Huber, Jacob, 46

Hudson River, 60

Hudsonville, Michigan, 76

Hull, William J., 92-93, 95-96

Huntington, Sam, 96

Huron House, 52-53

Illinois, 60, 76, 95, 102, 108

Illinois National Guard, 85

Illinois State Legislature, 102

Indiana, 38, 60, 76, 110

Indiana Harbor, Indiana, 79, 81

Interstate Commerce Act, 11

Interstate Commerce Commission, 47-49

Iron County, Michigan, 57

Iron River, Michigan, 57

Isaacson, Elmer, 85

J. Oswald Boyd, steamer, construction of, 78; early ocean service, 78; arrival on Great Lakes, 78-79; grounding of, 79; early salvage attempt, 80; crew abandoning of, 80-81; abandonment to underwriters, 81; investigation into grounding of, 82-83; explosion of, 84-85; unauthorized gasoline salvage from, 86-88; salvage of, 88-89; scrapping of, 89

Jackson, Michigan, 101

Jahn, Adolph, 5

Jerome, George H., 7

Judson Mine, 57

Kalamazoo, Michigan, 26, 102-104, 106-109

Kalamazoo County, Michigan, 8

Kaltschmidt, Albert, 121-122

Kansas, 76

Kansas City, Missouri, 99

Kansas-Nebraska Act, 101

Keenan, James J., 5

Keenan & Jahn furniture store, 1-3, 5-6

Kenosha, Wisconsin, 76

Kentucky, 66, 76

Keweenaw Peninsula, 28, 32

Keweenaw Waterway, 28-29, 31

Kirchberg, Winterhalter, & Keenan furniture house, 5

Kraus, Stanley E., 22

LaBelle, yacht, 83
Lake Carriers Association, 90
Lake Erie, 9, 24, 60
Lake Huron, 50, 61, 68, 71, 79, 89
Lake Michigan, 9, 23, 35, 38, 73, 76,
 79-80, 83-84, 86-87
Lake St. Clair, 20, 61, 79, 89
Lake Superior, 28, 33, 68
LaSalle, Michigan, 41
Lavadoux, Michel, 63
Law, Warner, 94
Leatherman, Charles, 42, 47-48
Liberty V12 Engine, 20
Lincoln, Abraham, invitation to
 Kalamazoo, 102-103; arrival in
 Kalamazoo, 104; speech at political
 rally, 105-107; departure from
 Kalamazoo, 107, as president, 108;
 death of, 108
Litchfield, Illinois, 11
Litchfield Car Company, 11-12
Lockheed Constellation, airliner, 98
Lockwood, James K., 50-51
Longyear, John M., 57
Los Angeles, California, 78
Louisiana Purchase, 62
Luening, Fred W., 71-72

M. M. Drake, steamer, 33
Mack, Andrew, 62
Mackinac County, Michigan, 88
Mackinac Island, 70, 80
Mackinaw City, Michigan, 79-80
Maki, Jacob, 58
Mansion House Hotel, 62
Margaret Yorke, tug, 123
Marold II, mail boat, 83-86, 90
Marquette, Michigan, 66-68

Marysville, Michigan, 83
Mastodon Iron Company, 57
Maumee River, 41
MBS International Airport, 100
McCauley, William W., 88
McCoy, Isaac, 73
McDonough, Bruce, 84
McElmurray, Leslie E., 4
McLeod, Albert, 88
McLeod, William, 88
Mecosta County, Michigan, 9
Menominee Iron Range, 56-57
Menominee River, 56
Michigan, barge, 33
Michigan Central Railroad, 8, 104
Michigan City, Indiana, 108
Michigan Exchange, 5
Michigan Fish Commission, 7-8, 11-14
Michigan Fisheries Visitors Center, 17
Michigan Lakeshore Railroad
 Company, 38
Michigan State Legislature, 7, 11, 14,
 51, 73
Michigan State Police, 94
Michigan Territory, 60, 64
Midland, Michigan, 91, 95, 100
Miltibarger, Katherine, 36
Milwaukee, Wisconsin, 23, 39, 71
Mineral Range Railroad Company, 29
Mining World Company, 57
Minneapolis, Minnesota, 23, 76
Minnesota, 56, 76
Minor, John S., 50
Minter, tugboat, 38
Miss Grand Rapids, aircraft, 18
Mississippi, 76
Mississippi River, 60, 62
Missouri, 60, 76
Mitchell, William B., 82
Monroe, Michigan, 40-42, 44-47
Morrison, John, 37-38

Index

Mount Clemens, Michigan, 19
Mt. Elliot Cemetery, 5-6
Muskegon, Michigan, 38
Muskegon River, 9
Mutual Transit Company, 29

Narsarssuak, Greenland, 90
National Air Transport, 26-27
Nebraska, 76
New Buffalo, Michigan, 38
New England, 73
New Jersey, 83, 92, 95, 102
New York, 47, 95
New York City, New York, 5, 26-27,
    60, 78
Newark, New Jersey, 92
Newark Airport, 92
Newell, John B., 4
Newhall, Wilson, 85
Newport, Michigan, 41, 43-44
Nicholson-Universal Steamship
    Company, 78, 80-81
Niles, Michigan, 7-8
Niles Road, 35
North Atlantic, 90
Northern King, steamer, 30
Northern Steamship Company, 33
Northern Wave, steamer, collision with
    bridge, 30-31; damage to, 32;
    construction of, 33; rescue of crew
    from sinking vessel, 33; ocean duty
    and scrapping of, 34;

O'Rourke, Patrick, 4
Oden State Hatchery, 17
Ohio, 24, 26, 35, 40, 66, 77, 95
Oklahoma, 77
Oldfield, John, 50
Owen, Willis, 40, 42-49

P. Hufnagle & Co., 5
P-47 Thunderbolt, aircraft, 91
Pack, Albert, 53
Pagel, John W., 3
Paisley, Scotland, 78
Pallaora, Victor, 58
Pan American Petroleum & Transport
    Company, 78
Panic of 1873, 29, 56
Panic of 1893, 57
Paquette, Antoine, 68-69
Paris, France, 62
Paris, Michigan, 9, 16
Paris hatchery, 9, 16
Pennsylvania, 95, 102
Pere Marquette Railway, 14
Petoskey, Michigan, 17
Petroleum Carriers Limited, 78
Philadelphia, Pennsylvania, 101, 118
Phyllis Yorke, tug, 123
Picklands Mathers & Co., 57
Pilkey, William, 81
Pioneer, steamer, 36
Pleasant Prairie, Wisconsin, 76
Point Edward, Ontario, 110-111
Pokagon hatchery, 8-9
Pokagon rail station, 8
Pontiac, Michigan, 62
Port Huron, Michigan, 50, 83, 110-112,
    114, 116-118, 120, 123-124
Port Huron Railroad Tunnel
    Company, 111
Portage Canal, 28
Potter Brothers Hardware Store, 53-54
Power, Albert L., 52
Printz, Mrs. Edward, 76
Prudden, George, 19
Public Act No. 124, 7

Quincy Smelter, 29

R. H. Fyfe Shoe Company, 6
Radaovitch, Dimitar, 58-59
Rambler, mail boat, 83
Raritan, tugboat, 90
Raymond, Earl, 97
Rentschler, Frederick B., 25
Republican Party, 50, 101-102, 106
Richard, Gabriel, 62-64
Ripon, Wisconsin, 101
River Clyde, Scotland, 78

River Rouge, Michigan, 41
Rochester, Michigan, 62
Rockwood, Michigan, 41, 43-44
Rooney, W. E., 46
Rosenthal, Joseph, 46

Saginaw, Michigan, 67-68, 91, 94-95, 100
Saginaw Air Traffic Communication, 93
Saginaw County Sheriff Department, 94
Saginaw County, Michigan, 91
Saintes, France, 62
Sandwich, Ontario, 46, 64
Sarnia, Ontario, 110, 112, 114, 117, 120, 123-124
Saugatuck, Michigan, 38
Saugatuck Point, 9
Sault Ste. Marie, 66, 68-69, 71-72, 80, 82, 86, 88, 90
Schlegel, Andrew, 42, 45, 47-48
Schoolcraft, Henry, 12
Scotia II, barge, 123
Selfridge Field, 19, 88
Seymour, Lester D., 27
Sherman House, 52-53
Shields, Robert, 31
Simmons Reef, 79, 81-82, 84-86, 88-90

South Bend, Indiana, 26
South Carolina, 39
Southworth, Charles T., 46
Springfield, Illinois, 102, 108
Springwells Township, 61
St. Clair, Michigan, 50
St. Clair, barge, 123
St. Clair Frontier Tunnel Company, 111
St. Clair River, 61, 79, 89, 110-111, 113-114, 116, 118, 120, 123-124
St. Clair Tunnel Company, formation of, 111; early contract awarded by, 112; construction of St. Clair Tunnel, 113-117; dedication ceremonies planned by, 117; acquisition of steam locomotives, 118; construction of powerhouse, 120; acquisition of electrically-powered locomotives, 120-121; acquisition by Canadian National Railways, 123
St. Clair Tunnel, requirement for, 110-111; early survey work, 112; design of, 113-114; construction of, 114-118; construction techniques and materials used, 114-116; alignment of tunneling shields, 116; dedication of, 117; dangers of toxic fumes, 118-119; accidents in, 119-120; electrification of, 120-121; attempted sabotage of, 121-122; acquisition by Canadian National Railways, 123; closure of, 124.
St. Ignace, Michigan, 70-71
St. Joseph, Michigan, 35-39
St. Joseph City Cemetery, 39
St. Joseph River, 36
St. Joseph Township, Michigan, 39
St. Lawrence River, 34, 78
St. Marys River, 69, 71-72, 80, 89

149

Index

St. Paul, Minnesota, 19, 23
ST-1, bomber, 19
Standale, Michigan, 76
Star Hotel, 52
Starr, Thomas I., 108
Ste. Anne Church, 62-64
Stevens, E. E., 4
Stocks, F. E., 4
Stone, Livingston, 8
Stony Creek, Michigan, 41
Stout, William Bushnell, 19, 21, 23, 26
Stout Air Services, early operations,
    18-21; suspension of Grand Rapids
    route, 22; opening of Cleveland
    route, 22-23; use of Ford Tri-Motor,
    23-24; sightseeing service, 24;
    growth of, 25; acquisition by
    United Aircraft, 25; opening of
    Chicago route, 25-26; expansion of,
    26; acquisition by National Air
    Transport, 26-27; dissolution of, 27
Stout Metal Aircraft Company, 19,
    20-21, 23
Straits of Mackinac, 79, 85

Tellier, Paul M., 124
Tennessee, 77, 95
Texas, 95
The Exchange Bank, 52
Thunder Bay, Lake Huron, 50
Thunder Bay Island, 50
Thunder Bay River, 50-51
Toledo, Ohio, 26-27, 40-42, 44, 46
Toledo & Monroe Railway, 41
Toledo Strip, 66
Toronto, Ontario, 118
Towle, Thomas, 19, 23
Traverse City, Michigan, 14
Trenton, Michigan, 41
Tri-City Airport, 91-94, 97-99

Trio, schooner, 38
Trombley, Frank F., 88
Tyler, Henry Whatley, 111-112, 117

U.S. Army, 60, 71, 85, 88, 91
U.S. Bureau of Marine Inspection and
    Navigation, 82
U.S. Coast Guard, 79-81, 84-85, 90
U.S. Congress, 11, 101
U.S. Constitution, 106
U.S. Fish Commission, 8, 13
U.S. House of Representatives, 64, 102
U.S. Navy, 19
U.S. Post Office Department, 67
U.S. War Production Board, 89
Union Hotel, 53
United Aircraft and Transport
    Corporation, 25-26
United Airlines, 25, 100

Vandenberg, Hoyt S., 91
Vickers-Armstrongs Ltd., 92
Vickers Viscount, airliner, 91-94,
    97-100
Vulcan Mine, 56

War of 1812, 64
Washington D.C., 91, 108
Wells, Hezekiah, 102-104, 107
West Virginia, 95
Westbrook, George, 53
Westbrook, Mrs. George, 53
Western Menominee Range, 56
Westinghouse Electric &
    Manufacturing Company, 120
Whig Party, 101
Whitefish Point, 70
Whitney, J. D., 56
Whitney, Walter M., 79-83
Wiersma, Nellie, 74-75

William Livingstone, tugboat, 9
William Penn, steamer, 61
William Sooysmith & Company,
    112-113

Willow Run, Michigan, 91
Wills, C. Harold, 83
Winans, Edward B., 117
Wisconsin, 56-57, 60, 76-77, 95
Wisconsin Bridge and Iron Company,
    32
Wolverine, rail car, 15-17
Woodmere Scrap Iron and Metal
    Company, 89
Woodward Avenue, 1-3, 5
World War I, 18, 34, 59, 78, 121
World War II, 89-91, 122
Wright J-4 Whirlwind, engine, 23
Wyandotte, Michigan, 41

Ypsilanti, Michigan, 62

www.ingramcontent.com/pod-product-compliance
Lightning Source LLC
Chambersburg PA
CBHW022025090426
42739CB00006BA/284